Teresa's Bible studies are some of the best o̶ a way to teach biblical truth with profound winsome and relatable way. This resource is a treasure!

KAT ARMSTRONG, author of *No More Holding Back* and *The In-Between Place*

Teresa, my pink-haired theologian, I want to hug you for writing these studies. You have shared practical, personal, and challenging ways to make the Bible come alive. When a smart woman chases after the heart of God, we all win.

TRICIA LOTT WILLIFORD, author of *You Can Do This* and *Just. You. Wait.*

In a noisy world filled with opinion, it can be difficult to cut through the clutter to find the voice of God and His vision for our lives. Plus, let's face it . . . the Bible is both intriguing and, at the same time, intimidating. Teresa does a beautiful job of taking us into God's heart by walking us through His Word. Her guided studies are for any woman who is wrestling with a sense of direction and believing in her worth. By taking us through the Scriptures in a practical, personal, and powerful way, she equips us to own our *now* and step boldly into our *next*.

MARSHAWN EVANS DANIELS, Godfidence Coach, TV personality, reinvention strategist for women, founder of SheProfits.com

With a relatable voice, Teresa makes studying the Bible approachable for women at any stage of faith. The Get Wisdom Bible Studies are a 360-degree look at God's Word with historical contexts, word studies, hands-on application, and commentary for each day's devotion. The studies are timely with varied messages of practicing contentment, trusting God in hard times, and leading the next generation. Teresa is serious about knowing God and how His character changes His people—the reader is not only encouraged to learn but to *live* the truths in these Bible studies.

BAILEY T. HURLEY, author, blogger, and speaker

Get ready for a Bible study that breaks the mold. Self-proclaimed "Bible nerd" Teresa Swanstrom Anderson has a passion for Scripture that is contagious. But don't you dare think this is a nerdy approach to study. Her warm and approachable style feels like a conversation with a wise and humble friend. Along the way, she will challenge you to *pick up your Bible* as she weaves linguistics, history lessons, and personal stories around a passage. I can't wait to recommend this series to women in our church.

GREG HOLDER, lead pastor at The Crossing; author of *The Genius of One* and *Never Settle*

GET WISDOM BIBLE STUDIES

Finding Your Place in God's Story

Five Weeks with the Women in *Jesus' Lineage*

Teresa Swanstrom Anderson

NavPress

A NavPress resource published in alliance
with Tyndale House Publishers

NavPress is the publishing ministry of The Navigators, an international Christian organization and leader in personal spiritual development. NavPress is committed to helping people grow spiritually and enjoy lives of meaning and hope through personal and group resources that are biblically rooted, culturally relevant, and highly practical.

For more information, visit NavPress.com.

Visit the author online at HeyItsTeresa.com.

Finding Your Place in God's Story: Five Weeks with the Women in Jesus' Lineage

Copyright © 2022 by Teresa Swanstrom Anderson. All rights reserved.

A NavPress resource published in alliance with Tyndale House Publishers.

NavPress and the NavPress logo are registered trademarks of NavPress, The Navigators, Colorado Springs, CO. *Tyndale* is a registered trademark of Tyndale House Ministries. Absence of ® in connection with marks of NavPress or other parties does not indicate an absence of registration of those marks.

The Team:
David Zimmerman, Publisher; Caitlyn Carlson, Acquisitions Editor; Elizabeth Schroll, Copy Editor; Olivia Eldredge, Operations Manager; Libby Dykstra, Designer

Cover illustration by Libby Dykstra. Copyright © Tyndale House Ministries. All rights reserved.

Photographs on page vii are the property of their respective copyright holders, and all rights are reserved. Top © 2018 by Crystal Woodman-Miller; bottom left © 2020 by Christina Ceranna; bottom middle © 2021 by Christina Ceranna; bottom right © 2020 by Bryn Schult.

Interior illustration of headphones copyright © Rawpixel.com/Freepik. All rights reserved.

Author is represented by Jana Burson of The Christopher Ferebee Agency, www.christopherferebee.com.

Author photograph on back cover by Christina Ceranna, copyright © 2020. All rights reserved.

"The Seven Days of the New Creation" table from *Jesus and the Jewish Roots of Mary: Unveiling the Mother of the Messiah* by Brant Pitre, copyright © 2018 by Brant Pitre. Used by permission of Image Books, an imprint of Random House, a division of Penguin Random House LLC. All rights reserved.

Unless otherwise indicated, all Scripture quotations are from The ESV® Bible (The Holy Bible, English Standard Version®), copyright © 2001 by Crossway, a publishing ministry of Good News Publishers. Used by permission. All rights reserved. Scripture quotations marked AMP are taken from the Amplified® Bible, copyright © 2015 by The Lockman Foundation. Used by permission. www.Lockman.org. Scripture quotations marked CSB are taken from the Christian Standard Bible,® copyright © 2017 by Holman Bible Publishers. Used by permission. Christian Standard Bible® and CSB® are federally registered trademarks of Holman Bible Publishers. Scripture quotations marked MSG are taken from *The Message*, copyright © 1993, 2002, 2018 by Eugene H. Peterson. Used by permission of NavPress. All rights reserved. Represented by Tyndale House Publishers. Scripture quotations marked NIV are taken from the Holy Bible, *New International Version*,® *NIV*.® Copyright © 1973, 1978, 1984, 2011 by Biblica, Inc.® Used by permission. All rights reserved worldwide. Scripture quotations marked NLT are taken from the *Holy Bible*, New Living Translation, copyright © 1996, 2004, 2015 by Tyndale House Foundation. Used by permission of Tyndale House Publishers, Carol Stream, Illinois 60188. All rights reserved. Scripture quotations marked NRSV are taken from the New Revised Standard Version Bible, copyright © 1989 National Council of the Churches of Christ in the United States of America. Used by permission. All rights reserved worldwide. Scripture quotations marked VOICE are taken from The Voice,™ copyright © 2012 by Ecclesia Bible Society. Used by permission. All rights reserved.

Some of the anecdotal illustrations in this book are true to life and are included with the permission of the persons involved. All other illustrations are composites of real situations, and any resemblance to people living or dead is purely coincidental.

For information about special discounts for bulk purchases, please contact Tyndale House Publishers at csresponse@tyndale.com, or call 1-855-277-9400.

ISBN 978-1-64158-469-2

Printed in the United States of America

28	27	26	25	24	23	22
7	6	5	4	3	2	1

To the woman who thinks she's not enough

who lives in the margins

who feels too much

or too small

who thinks her story is too hard

and her life is too messy:

You are worthy.

You are needed.

You are loved.

Just as you are.

Rise up, dear friend.

Step into the story God is writing.

He's inviting you into great things.

Let's Connect

Take a few moments to be replenished . . .
so that you can pour into others.

 HeyItsTeresa.com

 @teresa.swanstrom.anderson

 GetWisdomBibleStudies.com

I can't wait to discover all God is doing in your life through this exploration of the women in Jesus' lineage. I'd love to see and read all about it! Post using the hashtag #findingyourplace on Instagram, Twitter, and/or Facebook so we can encourage one another as we go through this study.

Teresa

Get to know Teresa

Teresa Swanstrom Anderson is a blogger, author, speaker, and Bible study teacher. Teresa grew up in Seattle, but spent her middle school years in Guatemala and has a deep love for people in developing countries. Now living in Denver, Colorado, with her husband and six children, she spends her days wiping off sticky counters, Instagramming, and blogging at HeyItsTeresa.com. She is the author of *Beautifully Interrupted* and the Get Wisdom Bible Studies. Teresa is passionate about helping women study the Bible, say *yes* to God, lead wherever they are, and live for what really matters.

Contents

Introduction

Never walk away from Wisdom—she guards your life;
love her—she keeps her eye on you.
Above all and before all, do this: Get Wisdom!
Write this at the top of your list: Get Understanding!
Throw your arms around her—believe me, you won't regret it;
never let her go—she'll make your life glorious.
She'll garland your life with grace,
she'll festoon your days with beauty.

PROVERBS 4:6-9, MSG

As a society, we not only like instant gratification—we expect it. We have on-demand movies, Netflix, and Hulu. When our favorite artist releases a new album, we download it onto our phones. If we want a new book, we can get it on our Kindle or listen to it on Audible with a single click. Even two-day shipping seems too slow for us sometimes, doesn't it?

But here's the thing: Growing in our relationship with Christ isn't necessarily quick. There is no instant download to encountering God. We can't pull up into the Starbucks drive-through and leave minutes later with a full grasp of the Bible and what it says about God and means for our lives.

So if you want a bullet-points-only, CliffsNotes experience of the Bible, this study may not be for you. But don't let that freak you out! I get that life is busy, and I promise—we can engage deeply with God through His Word in the midst of everything we're doing without being overwhelmed.

If you are a woman whose life isn't perfect, who struggles balancing all aspects of life and wearing all the hats—but you have a genuine desire to grow in your relationship with Jesus in intentional ways that don't require hours a day—then welcome! I'm hopping up onto my chair and throwing confetti around because, my dear friend, you're exactly where you're supposed to be. Together we're going to see the pages of the Bible come alive—and see the God of the Bible become more a part of our everyday experience as a result.

WHY WE STUDY THE BIBLE

The last time Jesus showed Himself to His disciples after His resurrection, mere moments before His ascension, something happened that is crucial for us to remember as we approach the Bible together. Luke 24:44-45 says, "Then he said to them, 'These are my words that I spoke to you while I was still with you—that everything written about me in the law of Moses, the prophets, and the psalms must be fulfilled.' Then he opened their minds to understand the scriptures" (NRSV).

We should be encouraged: Jesus opened their minds to understand that everything written about Him in Scripture must be fulfilled—but I am certain this isn't the only time Jesus has given individuals unique understanding.

He may even give it to you.

But here's the thing: These men had heard Scripture all their lives. They were ordinary working-class men without higher education. Not one of them had gone to school to become a rabbi, and they did not own a scroll or Bible. Yet because Scripture was read every time these men went to worship and biblical stories were retold throughout their lives, this knowledge was deep within the recesses of their minds and hearts. From childhood, these disciples heard God's Word.

We can know something, however, without understanding it.

And that's where the disciples were operating from.

Jesus decided to use this moment before His ascension to turn the spigot, and all their previous knowledge, the buildup of years of knowing God's Word, poured out. Except now, with Jesus' hand on that faucet, everything they had learned and heard through the years suddenly made sense to them.

With the help of Jesus, knowledge was finally tied together with comprehension, and the disciples had a major aha moment.

Just like the disciples, we won't have aha moments every time we open the Bible, worship, or pray. We will have days or even weeks when we don't "feel" any big revelations or hear whispered promptings from the Lord.

Do you feel like you're reading the Bible wrong or even wasting your time without having those heartfelt or aha moments? If you're like me, you want those heart moments all the time. That's when we feel especially close to Jesus. But here's the thing . . . it's not about us. Reading the Bible is not about having God give us a warm fuzzy feeling. It's not to show us how to act and react; neither is it about Him speaking to us. Spending time in the Word is about learning who God is. It's about growing in knowledge of the Creator of the universe and our Lord and Savior. Period.

When I realized a few years ago that the Word of God is not about me but about Him, I was rocked. I realized every verse within every page is written with the intent of us learning more about God's character and love.

Every story, every illustration, and every law loops back around to teach us who He is.

The Bible obviously shares how we should live and who we should be as lovers of the Lord, but it does so in relation to who God is and how He views us. That's why, whether you've loved Christ for five minutes or five decades, I'm just thrilled to be walking through this study of God's Word with you. Together we get to learn more about who He is! As we continue spending time with Him both in the

Word and in prayer, we'll be more prepared to experience Him when He opens our minds like He did for the disciples.

BEFORE WE BEGIN

The Bible

When I was young, I loved collecting. Specifically, I collected bottle caps and napkins. It's okay, you can laugh—it's totally weird. I had boxes of party napkins. I just loved that they were all different, like little pieces of art. Looking back, it kind of makes sense—I love entertaining and setting a pretty table. I still collect those fun napkins so I'm always ready when someone comes over, but I've also begun to collect something else: Bibles.

Why Bibles? Well, the two-hundred-year-old ones passed down from my grandfather are admittedly pieces of art, but I also have shelves of current versions. Still scratching your head as to why I'd have more than one? Well, let me tell you: because different versions say things in different ways.

A great way of understanding Scripture is consulting various translations. Though these Bibles may be worded differently, they don't ultimately differ in meaning and intent, because they all come from the Greek and Hebrew languages the Bible was originally written in. Some translations are more literal in interpretation than others, however. For example, both *The Message* (MSG) and *The Voice* translation (VOICE) capture the tone and essence of the text, while the *New Revised Standard Version* (NRSV), *English Standard Version* (ESV), and *Amplified Bible* (AMP) translations are known to be more literal, emphasizing word-for-word accuracy, literary excellence, and depth of meaning. In other words, versions like *The Message* should be looked at as a reading Bible (almost like a commentary that illuminates the text), rather than as a literal Bible, which is better for deep study.

Don't feel like you need to be a crazy Bible-lady like me, with shelves full of varying translations. The great thing about the internet is you can simply find different versions online. I encourage you to download the Bible Gateway or YouVersion app on your phone or head to their sites on your laptop. Try out a few different versions, and see which ones resonate with you best. If you have a favorite Bible already, google what the Bible you're using is translated for. Is it written for tone and intended meaning? Or is it translated for literal, word-for-word interpretation? Is it a reading Bible or a studying Bible?

In many weeks of this study, we'll explore a reading version of the passage, such as *The Message*, *The Voice*, or *The Passion Translation*, which will help us grasp the thematic picture in more accessible language. As we break apart each passage and dive in deeper, we will use the literal translations, so make sure you have one at the ready. I'll include the text from the *English Standard Version*, but in most cases, you will need to reference your own Bible or the Bible app on your phone for the rest. Make sense? Great!

Commentaries and Resources

If we want to be bold women who love God deeply, we must be women of Scripture. We must love the Bible in a way that surpasses others' opinion and research. To become spiritually literate, we must become a student of the Word. Commentaries and books about the Bible are incredibly helpful, but we need to make sure we're not spending more time in books *about* the Bible than in the *actual* Bible.

To be clear, I'm not saying we shouldn't refer to sermons and use commentaries. It would be foolish not to take advantage of the wisdom of others whom we have deep respect for. God has most certainly given the gift of discernment in regard to unraveling the Scripture to unique individuals.

I often study with a commentary or two nearby (in fact, I currently have three opened here on my desk), but through the years, I've learned how important it is to make my own interpretation and have my own thoughts about a Scripture passage (even if it's mostly questions) before considering someone else's thoughts and interpretation. I need to make sure my first Guide is God, rather than humans.

The first thing I'd like us to do is turn to a resource that can help us wrestle with what we're actually reading in the Bible. As we sort through God's Word, we need to be curious about the meanings beyond simply our initial understanding. That's why, in addition to adding the Bible Gateway or YouVersion app onto your phone, I'd also like you to download the Blue Letter Bible (BLB). This is really important because we're going to reference it. All. The. Time.

All of these apps I'm recommending are free, but if you want to download only one, choose the BLB because it has Bible translation options in addition to lots of extra resources. We'll be using this app every day in this study because it allows us to easily dig into the languages of the Bible (the Hebrew and Aramaic, the languages in which the Old Testament was written, and Greek, the New Testament's language).

If your eyes are glazing over and you're beginning to rethink wanting to do our study because "Whaaat? Dissecting Greek and Hebrew sounds hard / boring / not for me"—I get it. But this is something you can do! And digging into the Bible on this level is how we learn to study for ourselves and not have a faith that is spoon-fed to us. We want to make sure we are learning God's truth, right? Not just someone else's thoughts!

The BLB will rock your world if you haven't used it before. It totally changed the way I study. I'll show you really quickly how it can do the same for you. First, let's open the app and click on the search icon at the top. Let's look up something random like Psalm 23. (By the way, depending on whether you're in the app or on the website, you may want to choose a different Bible translation that better aligns with the wording we're discussing in the study—the BLB has a few different options.) Read verse 1 and see what questions come to mind. *Hmmm . . . what does it mean,* I shall not want? *Like, I'll literally never want for anything if the Lord is my Shepherd?*

Now this is the fun part. We can figure out what these words mean in the original language so we can better comprehend what God wants us to understand! To get there, tap the number by verse 1. On the screen that pops up, tap on *Interlinear** (we'll be using this function a lot!). On the next screen, scroll down to the phrase or word that you're wanting to dig into—in this case, I shall not want.

You'll see that in the Hebrew the word is חָסֵר or *chacer*. What does that word mean? Go ahead and click on it to find out.

On the page that pops up, you'll find all sorts of information about this word: how to say it, what part of speech it is, what its synonyms are. My favorite sections on this page are *Strong's Definitions* and the *Gesenius' Hebrew-Chaldee Lexicon*.

Now, let's say that learning more about the word and its meaning didn't clear up our question. We've started to dig in ourselves and not simply accept someone else's explanation of a biblical passage—but since things are still a little unclear, let's head to the commentaries.

Navigate back to Psalm 23 and click on verse 1 again. This time click on the *Text Commentaries* option. Some of my favorites in the app are by Matthew Henry and C. H. Spurgeon, but look through all of them to find which ones are most helpful to you. For the purposes of our exploration, let's tap on Spurgeon's Psalm 23 commentary. Here's my takeaway from what he wrote: "I shall not want" means I may not possess all that I wish for, but I am given a spirit of contentment. After all, does God not feed the ravens and cause the lilies to grow? I know that His grace will be sufficient for me.

Other places where you can find cross-references, commentaries, and lexicons online are Bible Hub (biblehub.com) and Bible Study Tools (biblestudytools.com). So many discoveries and insights are just a click away! When you start researching word, context, and

---

* On iPhones, this is called *Interlinear/Concordance*; to get to this function on the website, click on *Tools* next to the verse first.

commentaries in your study of the Bible, that is often the beginning of more questions and jumping down bunny trails of more questions and research. But you know what? The point of spending time in the Bible isn't to check off a task and move on with our day. Second Peter 3:18 says, "But grow in the grace and knowledge of our Lord and Savior Jesus Christ. To him be the glory both now and to the day of eternity."

Spending time in the Word and with the Lord is about gaining wisdom and knowledge. So if you decide to bounce around even more than I do within these pages and go down bunny trails that I have yet to discover, do it! You can spend fifteen minutes on a passage of Scripture or fifteen days, months, or years. This is all for you and your relationship with Him!

HOW TO USE THIS STUDY

Who + How

There are several ways you can engage in this study. Here are some tips for each context:

1. *Individually*: If you're doing this on your own, that's great! Write in the margins, highlight sections where God seems to want to get your attention, star things, put big question marks in areas you'd like to dig into further. Get this book messy! This study is a conversation between you and the Lord, so freewrite throughout as you really dig into all the beautiful things He wants to chat with you about!

2. *One-on-One*: We grow most in community, so find a friend who would like to do the study with you! Perhaps you'll meet together every week over coffee or lunch. Or maybe you'll meet over the phone or virtually.

3. *In-Person Group*: If you are doing this study in a group setting,

such as a church Bible study or home group, still strive to be 100 percent honest and authentic in your answers. Often, when we're with other women, we're afraid that they might judge our struggles, anger, pain, or even questions we have for or about God. But when we hide our true selves, we won't see the spiritual, emotional, and relational growth that can come out of time with other people who love Jesus. Of course, if the conversation dives into particular sections or questions that you don't feel ready to share publicly, give yourself permission to not answer. But if the group feels safe and supportive, I encourage you to bring all of yourself—including your messiness. And remember—even when you're in a group, make sure to invest in your daily, personal study! Coming to the group time after careful engagement with the Scripture will help everyone flourish.

For more specific directions on how to use this study as a group, head to GetWisdomBibleStudies.com to download the PDF guide. This guide will map out how to use this resource in a five-week study and how to focus on questions and themes most beneficial for group discussion, as well as how to create and facilitate a healthy group.

4. *Virtual Group*: If you're not plugged into a group in your local context, why not start your own virtual group via Zoom, FaceTime, Skype, or another video-conference website and app? Or perhaps your friends are super busy and spread across the state or country (or world!), so finding an actual day and time to meet proves difficult. If this is the case, you can start your own Facebook group, decide who will facilitate, and start chatting about what you're learning each day or each week. You and your friends can simply post whenever works best for everyone's individual schedules! Sounds fun, right?

Each day of this study can take you only twenty to thirty minutes, but if you'd like to dig deeper, you'll be learning the skills to explore more deeply in the passage of Scripture and the context of the stories of these five extraordinary women in Jesus' family. At the end of each day, you'll be prompted into a time of journaling prayer, so you can talk to and hear from God as He helps you understand your place in His big story of redemption.

When + Where

Before starting this study, consider when in your day would best provide some uninterrupted time to dig in. I know finding time can be so difficult in our busy lives, thanks to jobs, kids, and other responsibilities. And fitting in Bible study five days a week can feel like a lot, particularly during busy seasons of life (for example, this study would be especially rich during Advent, and we know how crazy things can get then!). Because of that, this study has been intentionally crafted with only three days of study per week, to best fit your pace of life. You may want to do a Monday/Wednesday/Friday rhythm, or you may find that it's easier to do three days in a row. Whatever you decide to do, I promise that you'll still encounter depth and a transformative time in God's Word. We make time for the things that matter—and I promise, time meeting God through His Word is so worth it.

Personally, though I'm certainly not a morning person (hello, coffee), my brain is most attentive in the morning . . . plus, I really love having time with the Lord to center myself before the chaos of the day begins. Through the years, my family notices when I haven't done this for a few days—my joy, patience, and kindness just isn't what it usually is when I'm in the Word at the start of the day!

Simply can't get up any earlier than you currently do? Maybe you work shifts or have little ones not yet sleeping all the way through the night. I get it, and I've been there. I still encourage you to give God the firstfruits of your time, though. Throughout the Bible, we are encouraged to give the first and best to the Lord. And though we may not have a first crop of corn or a perfect lamb to present to Him, we certainly can give Him the first of our time—not the leftovers. Even if rising earlier in the morning feels impossible in this season, you can still offer Him your firstfruits. Pack a bag with your Bible and this study and do it at the beginning of your lunch hour at work, first break between classes, or the first moments of your child's naptime. The laundry, dishes, and showering can wait. Put Him first.

What You'll Need

This study is meant both to guide you through the lives of the women in Jesus' lineage and to equip you to forge your own path through God's Word so He can make it alive in your everyday life. As you begin your study, here are a few things to keep on hand:

- A Bible in your favorite translation
- Your phone with the Blue Letter Bible app and BibleGateway or YouVersion downloaded
- A pen (you'll find space to write as we explore the women of Jesus' lineage together, but also feel free to scribble in the margins as you need to!)
- A smartphone with internet access so you can watch the short videos that introduce each week (you can find those at GetWisdomBibleStudies.com).
- A place without distraction where you can truly dig in!

One Last Thing

A final note to remember as we go through this study: The Bible was written for us, but it's not written *to* us. The Bible is full of stories, poetry, laws, parables, and such, which were written for people who lived in a different culture thousands of years before any of us were born. So each week in this study, we're going to explore some of the behind-the-scenes aspects of Scripture. We're going to figure out the historical and cultural background. We'll try to learn the *why* of it all. We need to become not just readers of the Word . . . but *studiers* of it. Only then can we understand what God has *for* us in His Word.

FINDING YOUR PLACE IN GOD'S STORY

Waiting is never something we love. But anticipation? Anticipation is exciting. I mean, if my anniversary was approaching and I knew my husband and I were celebrating with a trip to Italy, I'd love the wait. I'd anxiously and excitedly count the moments (this has never happened, but hey, Ben, I'm putting it out there). That's a good wait. A fun wait. A wait with a light at the end of the tunnel—a timeline until something amazing happens.

The Bible is a bit like this. All throughout Scripture we read little hints, details, and prophecies about when the Messiah would arrive. No one knew the whens or hows about it, but God gave prophets insight that no one else had. From grandparent to parent to child, the words of the coming Messiah were passed down for thousands of years, and these recorded prophesies provided a road map of sorts. As God whispered signs and circumstances to the prophets, He foretold things humankind should anticipate while they waited. The writings of the Old Testament were completed in 450 BC (Jesus was born around 4 BC) and contains over three hundred prophecies. And Christ fulfilled every one of them. Mind-blowing, right?

> [19]He paid for you with the precious lifeblood of Christ, the sinless, spotless Lamb of God. [20]God chose him as your ransom long before the world began, but now in these final days, he has been revealed for your sake.
>
> 1 PETER 1:19-20, NLT

But amid all these prophecies were *people*. The pathway to Jesus was filled with human beings making choices, moving toward God and following Him in the middle of their everyday lives—as well as in the middle of tragic and traumatic circumstances. God's story for the salvation of the world would unfold through the lives of men and women who had no idea of the role they were playing at the time.

Only a handful of these people are named in the genealogy of Jesus . . . and only five of them are women. And this is a big deal. The culture of Jesus' day was patriarchal—that is, men were considered the most important and significant in someone's family line, and women were often regarded as property, not people.

And interestingly, even if women were named, wouldn't you expect them to be the women who did everything "right"? Who held places of honor and significance in the Hebrew Scriptures, like Sarah, Rebekah, or Leah?[1] Instead . . .

¹This is the genealogy of Jesus the Messiah the son of David, the son of Abraham:

²Abraham was the father of Isaac,
Isaac the father of Jacob,
Jacob the father of Judah and his brothers,
³Judah the father of Perez and Zerah, *whose mother was Tamar*,
Perez the father of Hezron,
Hezron the father of Ram,
⁴Ram the father of Amminadab,
Amminadab the father of Nahshon,
Nahshon the father of Salmon,
⁵Salmon the father of Boaz, *whose mother was Rahab*,
Boaz the father of Obed, *whose mother was Ruth*,
Obed the father of Jesse,

⁶and Jesse the father of King David.
David was the father of Solomon, *whose mother had been Uriah's wife . . .*
¹⁶and Jacob the father of Joseph, the husband of Mary, *and Mary was the mother of Jesus who is called the Messiah.*

MATTHEW 1:1-6, 16, NIV, EMPHASIS MINE

The five women named and honored in the genealogy of Jesus are not the expected matriarchs but the ones with hard, complicated stories. Perhaps they're the ones who best exemplify this prophecy from Isaiah:

On this humbled ground, a tiny shoot, hopeful and promising,
    will sprout from Jesse's stump;
a branch will emerge from his roots to bear fruit.

ISAIAH 11:1, VOICE

Some of these women form the roots and rings in the stump, and one is the embodiment of this "tiny shoot, hopeful and promising." But every one of these women is just like us: resoundingly ordinary, tainted by sin, and yet unexpectedly used to change the world when they found their place in God's story.

Take Joy,

Teresa

Tamar

A Woman Who Pursues What Is Right

WEEK 1 • *Day 1*

LISTEN

Place your phone over the QR code for this week's sacred song. Listen to it before you begin, or whenever you'd like, to prepare your heart.

READ GENESIS 38

It's snowing outside—the big, fluffy flakes that make you feel like you're living in a snow globe. We're in the early hours, those quiet moments that don't quite feel like night but aren't yet the bright day. My coffee and I sit in front of our picture windows, watching and waiting for the first streaks of brilliant light to climb atop the mountain. I'm anticipating the miracle of the morning sun, how those fluffy snowflakes will soon sparkle like glitter.

This is my favorite perch in our cabin: The desk in the loft with a panoramic view of the ski slopes where so many of our family memories have been made. We've affectionately named our cabin—a run-down condo at Copper Mountain that we're fixing up—our "Happy Place."

We waited nearly a decade to find this little place. We spend our winter weekends skiing, going to the little church in a grove of trees just off the lift at the top of a Blue run. As we gather to listen to the pastor's message, some of us stay clipped into our bindings, while others step off their snowboards or skis and leave them in the snow a few feet away. We all fumble with the bulletin through thick gloves or mittens, clumsily turning to the right page and belting out the same choruses and hymns I've sung since childhood, proclaiming God's glory and workmanship on this mountainside.

And now, after a wait of nearly ten years trekking up to the mountains for ridiculously long and exhausting day trips, we've finally found our small Happy Place.

Waiting is an inevitable part of life—and rarely easy. Ben and I have waited weeks for medical-test results, months for our runaway teen to return, years to step out of financial struggle. I'm guessing you've struggled through your own seasons of waiting too.

But waiting doesn't have to be something that just happens *to* us. If we find ourselves looking into the unknown, moving from one season of hard things into another, we're not helpless and we're not hopeless. The details of wait and struggle do not define who we are in the middle of it all. You see, there's a secret to waiting well. A pause or delay can turn into a moment to grow.

What does this all have to do with Tamar, you might ask? Well, we might be tempted to define her by her wait. Honestly, for years I misunderstood her story. Whether I had literally been taught or simply had been given the impression that Tamar was a conniving you-know-what who got impatient and couldn't just be content with where she was, I got it all wrong. I got *her* all wrong. (Tamar, I'm sorry. I can't wait to ask you a million questions in heaven.)

I'm not the only one who was mistaken. A lot of the commentaries I've researched got her wrong too. *She didn't trust God enough to wait for His full plan to be revealed!* they exclaim. *She took things into her own hands instead!* Through the ages, many have found it strange that the Lord would place a woman "like her" in Christ's genealogy; some even claimed it was proof that God can use even evil sinners for His purpose.

And yes, I agree that God can use anyone and all things will work together for His good (Romans 8:28). But I don't think that's what is going on with Tamar. After months of digging into her story, I've realized we're missing some big details. We're misunderstanding, misreading, and misinterpreting things with our twenty-first-century, Western perception of the world.

In the middle of her wait, Tamar saw right through the injustice around her. And she didn't just sit down and give up. She chose to do a brave, terrifying thing: to pursue justice and chase what is right no matter what. And she helps us see how to do the same—even when it means being unconventional and unorthodox. Sometimes the right thing doesn't look "right" to those around us . . . but God knows our hearts.

Don't just take my word for it—over the next three sessions, we're going to get to know this woman for ourselves . . . and realize how her example helps us understand our own place in God's story a little better.

1. After reading Genesis 38 in your favorite translation, pen down the essence of the story in a few short sentences:

2. What are your immediate thoughts about this story?

You may be like me, giving Tamar some serious side-eye for sleeping with her father-in-law, Judah. It seems a bit, well . . . yuck. And weird. And over-the-top. It sort of feels like she was acting in doubt and self-preservation.

But remember—being women who take God's Word seriously means we can't just take things at surface value. We need to look at the bigger picture.

3. Flip back to Genesis 15 and read verses 1-5. What did God promise Abraham?

4. What happened at the beginning of Genesis 16?

_____

_____

_____

Sarah was tired of waiting for God. He had told her what He was going to do, but she was getting impatient. Maybe she thought she missed it or understood Him wrong. Maybe she even wondered if YHWH needed her to fulfill His plan. So, without consulting Him about it, she went about trying to "help" His promise of a child come to pass.

Want to know how many times I've tried to "help" God along when I'm unhappy with His timing? About a million. Waiting is hard, particularly when we don't know if the wait will ever end. But it's during this time that God strengthens our character and our trust in Him.[1] Either we're going to trust God enough to go with Him, or we're not. We need to stop telling Him to hurry up and instead recognize that He's inviting us into His own story—and what He does in us in the waiting is part of that.

Sarah's son, Isaac, was a long time coming—twenty-five years, in fact, after God first spoke to her husband, Abraham (Genesis 12:4, 21:5). Twenty-five years to develop Sarah's trust in God, to allow her to test that trust, to show her the richness of dependence and the pain of choosing her own way. Twenty-five years to do something miraculous, to show Sarah that only God could give her this miracle. Maybe, just maybe, God took all that time to shape her into the woman and mother and God follower He wanted to raise Isaac. Who we are, who God shapes us to be, affects all the generations that follow.

But first Sarah had to experience the consequences of impatience and doubting God.

Was this what Tamar was doing? Trying to "help" God because she was tired of waiting?

5. Do you think Tamar and Sarah were similar in their motivations? Why or why not?

6. What did Judah say of Tamar in Genesis 38:26? Does this surprise you?

Righteous. Wow. That's a pretty big statement, especially from someone who was just about to burn his daughter-in-law to death for "prostitution" (38:24, NIV).

Time to do some digging into the original language so we can figure out what's actually going on here. Let's open up the Blue Letter Bible (BLB) app on our phones and dig into this a bit.

7. Head to Genesis 38:26 in the Blue Letter Bible (BLB) app (now is a great time to download it if you haven't yet!). Click on the verse, then tap on *Interlinear* and scroll down to the word *righteous* (or whatever the comparable word is in the version you're looking at). Once you've tapped on the link for *ṣāḏaq* (צָדַק, pronounced *tsa-dak*), scroll down to the *Outline of Biblical Usage* and see exactly how the word *righteous* is translated. Write down several of the descriptions below:

Judah wasn't simply saying Tamar wasn't sinful and disgraceful . . . he was placing blame upon himself, saying *he* was the guilty party, not her. He's exclaiming that he is in the wrong and is the one who is punishable, not her. By saying she is righteous, he declares Tamar upright in morality, affirming that she did what was honorable and just.

 History Lesson

Judah's father, Jacob, is Abraham's grandson; patriarch of the Jewish faith; and father of the twelve sons whose families would become the twelve tribes of Israel.

Judah gave Tamar (who was in the guise of a temple prostitute) his signet ring, cord, and staff as a guarantee of future payment—and in reality, as a sign of his sin. When she returned it, this tangible sign of his unrighteousness caused Judah to repent.

The next time we see a reference to Judah's staff in Genesis, something interesting is happening. In Genesis 49, Jacob is making prophecies on his deathbed. As his sons gather around to hear his last words, Jacob has a message for each of them . . . and verse 10 gives us a particularly pertinent statement about Judah:

> The scepter shall not depart from Judah,
>   nor the ruler's staff from between his feet,
> until tribute comes to him;
>   and to him shall be the obedience of the peoples.

8. What do you think this prophecy means? How does it point to Jesus?

As pastor and author Tony Evans shares in his commentary,

> Joseph was Jacob's favorite, and I think he would have
> been Jacob's personal choice to continue the messianic line.
> But God had chosen Judah—in spite of his failings—to
> father the line of kings leading to Christ, as the scepter will
> not depart from Judah or the staff from between his feet
> until he whose right it is comes (49:10). He would be the
> new leader of his brothers, full of power and majesty like
> a lion (49:8-9). From Judah would come the kingly line
> of David and Solomon and all of their descendants. More
> importantly, Jesus would be called "The Lion from the tribe
> of Judah" (Rev 5:5).[2]

Both the scepter and staff are symbols of power and authority.
Most of Judah's life was full of regret and running from God—and,
perhaps, abdicating that authority through his own unrighteousness
in giving his staff to Tamar.

It wasn't until he received the staff back from her that Judah
became a man of honor. It wasn't until he laid down the physical
sign of his tarnished authority and accepted it back in repentance
that God bestowed true authority on him. That authority would not
depart from him and his family again.

For her part, Tamar took hold of the staff with its inherent
symbolism that God gave her (through a sinful Judah), and as she
used it to demonstrate her righteousness, we see the authority and
power extend to her as well. God bestowed an overlooked, mistreated
woman with honor and authority that would never diminish. Many
nations would be born from Judah, but just as many would be born
from Tamar. One could say she held the scepter and was grafted into
the family through it.

As Pulitzer Prize–winning author of *The Color Purple* Alice Walker
so famously said, "The most common way people give up their power

is by thinking they don't have any." (Woo! Say it again for the ladies in the back, Ms. Walker!) Satan often makes us believe we have no power, doesn't he? But God sees. God knows. And He offers the powerless His power and authority. He gave Tamar far more influence and place in His bigger story than she ever could have dreamed.

We've just scratched the surface of Tamar's story, and we're going to learn more about her in the days to come. But as we wrap up today, let's remember that this first woman named in Jesus' family line was called righteous for standing up to unrighteousness. That her patience and faithfulness in the face of injustice, and her participation in God's work to turn Judah toward righteousness, pointed toward the One who would come to right injustice and bring His people to repentance.

My friend Vivian Mabuni says in her book *Open Hands, Willing Heart*:

> We may not have the opportunity to see the direct outcome
> of our choices or live the life we always dreamed of, but
> God maps out for us a way to walk in freedom from our
> expectations of how we think life should unfold, even when
> our circumstances don't make sense to us.[3]

No more sitting back and shutting down, thinking we have no power. In God's power, we can fight injustice, we can right wrongs, and we can continue stepping forward into the story He is writing us into.

> Justice is what love looks like in public.[4]
> CORNEL WEST

Take a moment to lay before God what you're feeling stuck in or wronged by, and ask Him to show you how these are an invitation to step into His power and story.

_____

_____

_____

_____

_____

_____

_____

_____

_____

Amen.

WEEK 1 • *Day 2*

LISTEN
Place your phone over the QR code for this week's sacred song.

READ GENESIS 37:1–38:2

Amy Purdy was only nineteen when she found herself fighting an inexplicable and aggressive form of bacterial meningitis. As the blood disease spread quickly, doctors gave her a 2 percent chance of survival and immediately placed her on life support. Over the next two and a half months, she would lose both her legs, her kidneys, her spleen, and the hearing in her left ear. But she fought—hard. And slowly, miraculously, Amy grew stronger.

But after all that fighting, when she was finally well enough to try prosthetic legs . . . that's when reality set in. Life was different. *She* was different. And she had a choice: Would she give in to the exhaustion—or would she continue to face the hard things in front of her?

Amy asked herself,

If my life were a book, and I was the author of that book, how would I want this story to go? I saw myself walking gracefully. And I saw myself somehow helping other people through my journey, and I saw myself snowboarding again. . . . I could feel the wind against my face and the beat of my racing heart as if it was happening at that very moment. And that passion, and that fire I felt inside, that is when a new chapter of my life began.[5]

Four months after she lost her legs, she was back up on a snowboard. She worked with her legmaker to create new legs that would help her fly down mountains. And Amy Purdy went on to be the first female to win a bronze medal in Paralympic snowboarding.

"I learned it's that change and it's that challenge that forces us to figure out what we're really made of," she said. "It makes us dig deep. It makes us find our fire."[6]

When we're faced with the unexpected, the hard, the overwhelming—that's when we find what we're really made of. The choices we make when it's easier to just give up show who we really are. When there's nothing left to hide behind, the real you steps forward.

That's our girl Tamar. Everything had been stripped away—and who she was emerged from the darkness. But we won't understand the depths of her story and the reality of the choices she made unless we take a close look at the contrast Scripture provides us: the person who made a different set of choices. That's why we're going to talk about Judah quite a bit today. After all, one story isn't complete without details from another. As we'll learn, Judah was a guy who wasn't interested in putting in the hard work to become a man of honor and good character. For many years, he forgot who he was and Whose he was—and he experienced the fallout of that choice.

I've been there. Maybe you have too. When we take our eyes off the One we're following and who He's calling us to be, life may feel easier in the short term . . . but it gets a lot harder in the end.

1. After reading Genesis 37 and the first several verses of chapter 38, what words would you use to describe Judah?

_____

_____

_____

 History Lesson

Abraham → Isaac → Jacob → Judah

As we mentioned in day 1, Judah's father, Jacob, is the grandson of Abraham. Like Judah, Jacob was cunning and deceitful—and he devastated his brother's life. Tricking his ailing and blind father (Isaac), Jacob stole the blessing and birthright intended for Esau (Genesis 27). Because Esau planned to kill Jacob in revenge, Isaac summoned Jacob and instructed that he travel to his mother's family to find a wife and start a family. (Side note: Isaac specifically commanded in Genesis 28:1 that Jacob not marry a Canaanite. More on that later.)

Upon traveling to Haran and finding his mother's brother Laban, Jacob saw Laban's daughter Rachel, who was a shepherdess. It was love at first sight. Jacob agreed to work for Laban for seven years in order to receive Rachel's hand in marriage. (Remember, during this time, women were commodities, used as pawns in business deals.) Like the soap opera that much of the Old Testament is, Laban tricked Jacob at the wedding, and without realizing it, Jacob married Rachel's older sister Leah instead. Can you imagine how his stomach must have dropped when he eventually lifted her veil? But because it was Rachel that he loved, Jacob worked seven additional years to also marry Rachel. (Sister-wives. Yikes.)

Genesis 29:31-35 tells us that the Lord saw how Leah was neglected, and He opened her womb to conceive four sons (and, we read in Genesis 30:21, one daughter, Dinah). The first three sons (Reuben, Simeon, and Levi) were named from Leah's pain (for example, Reuben means, "The LORD has seen my affliction; surely my husband will love me now," (Genesis 29:32, CSB). But by the time Judah was born, Leah's heart was positioned differently. In verse 35, she says, "This time I will praise the LORD"—and so she named him Judah.

In ancient Israelite culture, not having children wasn't an option. Women's sole purpose in life was to bear children, specifically male offspring. Not being able to do so was devastating, just as it is today. But along with the heartbreak of loss came painful cultural stigma as well. No children meant shame. It meant there was no one to care for them as they grew old. Women without children would become destitute. They would have nothing and would likely starve to death in their poverty. And without a male descendant, an entire family's heritage would be erased from history.

Because Rachel was terrified that her sister was conceiving and she was not, she used her servant as a pawn, a placeholder to bear children for her. Eventually, the Lord opened Rachel's womb as well, but meanwhile, Leah also brought her servant into the equation. This woman bore more children for "Leah's side" as the sisters competed for their husband's love through their children.

Joseph, who was around seventeen when his brothers sold him to Ishmaelite traders, was his father's favorite because he was the first son from Jacob's beloved Rachel, who died giving birth to her second son, Benjamin.

JACOB'S FAMILY

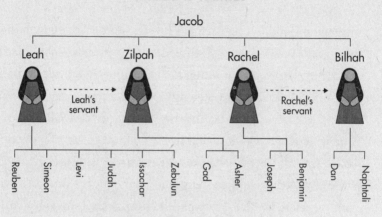

2. On the fateful day when Joseph was sold and trafficked into slavery, what did Judah say to his brothers (see Genesis 37:26)?

Judah may not have encouraged killing Joseph like several of his other brothers prompted, but he certainly didn't stand up for justice, either. This is a stark contrast to the woman who would eventually become his daughter-in-law—a woman who stood for justice even when it nearly destroyed her reputation and her life.

Why are we looking at Judah's response to Joseph? Because Tamar's story seems awkwardly plopped down right in the middle of Joseph's. We read about how he was sold to Potiphar, an officer of Pharaoh, then *boom* . . . we're taken out of the story abruptly.

3. What do we learn about Judah in verse 1 of Genesis 38?

_____

_____

_____

We're not told how much time passed between when Joseph was sold and when Judah left his father's house, but commentaries theorize that Judah was around age fifteen or sixteen when he departed from his family and settled among the Canaanites.[7] I wonder if Judah felt extreme shame and guilt seeing his father every day, knowing Jacob was mourning a son's death when Joseph was actually alive . . . or was he? Judah had no idea what had happened to his brother once they sold him. Maybe the regret and disgrace were too much for him—yet he didn't have the strength of character to come out with the truth. Perhaps he self-sabotaged and ran away—away from his family and from the God they followed.

4. Why do you think Tamar's story is placed in the middle of Joseph's story? What does it indicate to you about Judah in comparison (or in contrast) to Joseph and Tamar?

_____

_____

_____

The land of Canaan was full of idols, child sacrifice, and a lifestyle completely opposite from what God was leading Israel toward. And yet Judah distanced himself from the faith of his father and moved to the land he knew was opposed to everything his family believed in. Rather than allowing his father to select a suitable wife for him, as was tradition, Judah settled in Canaan, choosing his own bride. Over and over, Judah chose to flee justice, to shun honor; Tamar and Joseph stood up for what was right at great personal cost.

We may not be told much about what Judah did in Canaan, but the impact of his choices speaks loudly. After marrying the daughter of a man named Shua, Judah had three sons: Er, whom Judah named himself, and Onan and Shiloh, whom Judah's wife named.

5. Why do you think Judah named his first son but not his second and third sons?

I'm going to be honest—I originally made some assumptions based on Judah's presence in naming his first son but not his other two. Was he simply abdicating his role, handing the reins over to a woman not from the people of God? But then God nudged me, reminding me what we're studying here: that each of the women mentioned in Jesus' lineage was unexpected, and we can't assume or judge or go for the easy answer. After all, Tamar also came from this land. We don't know much about Judah's wife. And a woman naming her children in this time was not unusual; in fact, the Hebrew Bible gives twenty-three examples of mothers naming their children, versus eighteen times a father had named the child.[8] (Strangely, the only documented time parents named the children together was in Genesis 25:25-26 when Isaac and Rebekah named Jacob and Esau.)

So apparently, we shouldn't be reading into why Judah didn't name every one of his sons . . . or should we?

6. Let's head to the BLB and take a look at the meaning of each of their names:

Er (Genesis 38:3):

Onan (Genesis 38:4):

Shelah (Genesis 38:5):

Now, we don't want to read something into the pages of Scripture that isn't there. But let's consider each of these names in the context of what we do know:

- what we know about Judah and his wife;
- the fact that Judah was present for one name but not the others;
- what each of these names means; and
- the actions of each of these children as adults.

In Scripture, names have meaning. While we can't know definitively the purpose of these names, we can ask God to give us some clarity as we dig deeply into His Word.

7. Based on everything we know, what might be some reasons each of these children was given their name?

One thing seems sure: Judah's faithlessness and lack of spiritual leadership had a direct impact on the kinds of men his sons became.

8. What does the Scripture we're digging into this week seem to indicate about Judah's faith and character? Why?

_____

_____

_____

_____

Palestinian scholar Jean Zaru says, "Many argue that one's faith, or one's spirituality, is one's own private affair. I disagree, for spirituality includes all the dimensions of human, personal, and societal living that combine to make human life human—the measure of the fullness of God's gift."[9] In other words, your faith should be notably personal, but never private (see Matthew 5:15). Judah's family had a direct relationship with the one true God. He was generations into a lineage of faith. But none of that reality shows up in his actions or relationships prior to Genesis 38:26:

- Judah may have swayed his younger brothers away from killing Joseph, instead convincing them to sell Joseph to Ishmaelite traders who were headed to Egypt, but he didn't keep Joseph safe.
- Judah walked away from his family, his closest earthly connection to God.
- Judah married a Canaanite, in direct defiance of the counsel his grandfather Isaac had given his father Jacob.
- Judah didn't stay in the land where God had placed his family; instead, he dwelt among people who worshiped idols and hated God.

Enter Tamar, a Canaanite girl whose father gave her in marriage to Judah's eldest son, Er. We learn quickly in Genesis 38 that Er was "wicked in the sight of the LORD" (verse 7).

We don't know how long Tamar was married to Er, but no child resulted from their marriage. As we saw in the story of Rachel and Leah, not producing an heir created a precarious future for a woman. Tamar's wait to conceive would have been demoralizing. According to the custom of the time, she was responsible for providing a son to carry on Er's family line. From what little we know about her husband, we can guess that he wasn't particularly understanding about her "failure" to do so. Tamar's marriage couldn't have been a happy one.

Whatever wickedness Er embraced, it must have been next level, because God "put him to death" for it (Genesis 38:7). And, it seems, Judah just stood by, watching his son's wickedness. He hadn't kept his brother Joseph safe, and protecting his daughter-in-law Tamar doesn't seem to have been a priority either.

Tamar was the victim of profound injustice, and—as we'll see in our next session—it was only going to get worse. At this point in her story, she seems to be a bystander, powerless to advocate for herself. That was the reality for so many women in the ancient world. But what makes it particularly painful for Tamar is that the family she married into *should* have been different. Judah knew what it was to live rightly. He could have married a woman who would advocate for her daughter-in-law. He could have raised his sons to follow the God of his fathers. He could have demanded they treat Tamar with integrity. All of this he could have done, and he chose not to. So, as we'll see, this woman—born outside God's chosen people and treated as worthless—pursued justice. At the risk of great personal cost, she did what Judah would not.

9. Who in your life seems powerless? How can you choose to live rightly and advocate for them?

If you are feeling powerless, subject to the whims and choices of people who are choosing wrongly, you may be experiencing a lot of grief. When it seems like there's no way out, you can feel despair. But don't. God sees you. He knows. And God beckons you forward. As you do the next right thing, He'll be beside you.

God understands that life is hard. But He also knows that justice and healing and hope come from walking through, not around. He knows that we find restoration by stepping forward with Him into the hard stuff. Judah's avoidance shows us that choosing not to face things only creates more pain. Only when we do the hard work and pursue what is right will our hearts begin to be made whole.

If you're sitting here today with unforgiveness from pain inflicted on you, you can change that. It's better to face the hurt and forgive. When you avoid your hurt or run away from it, those feelings cascade into more deeply entrenched bitterness. Don't let the sun go down on one more day without releasing those feelings to the Lord and being authentic with Him in it all. He can handle the anger, the disappointment, and the pain. Bring it to Him.

> Sometimes the best, most life-giving way to lead is by
> suffering well. Sometimes the best, most life-giving way to
> lead is by refusing to allow death, mourning, crying, or pain
> to dictate the story line of our lives and history.[10]
> SCOTT SAULS

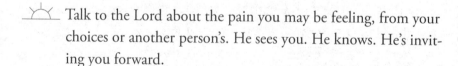 Talk to the Lord about the pain you may be feeling, from your choices or another person's. He sees you. He knows. He's inviting you forward.

Amen.

WEEK 1 • *Day 3*

LISTEN
Place your phone over the QR code for this week's sacred song.

READ GENESIS 37

*We like to think of our champions and idols as superheroes who were
born different from us. We don't like to think of them as relatively
ordinary people who made themselves extraordinary.*

CAROL DWECK

In 1775, the Cherokee and Creek tribes clashed at what would later be called the battle of Taliwa. Seventeen-year-old Nanye'hi[11] hid nearby, "chewing the lead bullets for [her husband's] rifle to make them more deadly."[12] But when her husband fell in battle, she moved into action. Nanye'hi "sprang up from behind a log and rallied the Cherokee warriors to fight harder. Taking up [his] rifle, she led a charge that unnerved the Creeks and brought victory to the Cherokees."[13]

After that day, Nanye'hi was called Agi-ga-u-e ("Beloved Woman") and became a leader among her people.[14] She was a fierce advocate for her tribe keeping their land, while at the same time pursuing peacemaking and cooperation with white settlers. She even used her position to save a white captive from being murdered.

When Nanye'hi picked up her husband's rifle from his suddenly still hands, she was faced with the same decision Tamar and the other women named in Jesus' lineage had to make: victim or victor? Would she step back and accept what was, or move forward into what could be? She had no idea that day would be the beginning of her leadership within her tribe and people, but she stepped out, taking her place in a larger story.

Throughout Scripture, we read of God's promise to continue the lineage of Abraham, Isaac, and Jacob—and the lineage of faith He called them to—through many generations. This is one of the main themes of the book of Genesis, and Tamar's story is a central example. None of the people in this story understood God's long-term plan for the Israelites. They could see only their own story, their own circumstances. Few of us look outside our own story, but the women in Jesus' family remind us to stop and ask ourselves: Will we step back or move forward? Will we pursue what is right, believing that more is happening than we can see? God had a much bigger plan. He is always, always telling a larger story.

But still—how do we make sense of what Tamar does? How can her actions fit into God's larger story? Well, first, it's important for us to remember that while the Bible was written *for* us, it wasn't written *to* us. We're not Israelites living thousands of years ago, and this story wouldn't have been confusing to the ancient Hebrew people like it is to us. This is why it's important for us to dig into culture, history, and the original language the Bible was written in.

1. We learn first in Genesis 38:8 and then again in 38:11 that there was tradition meant to protect the family line of a deceased man. What is this tradition?

History Lesson

The custom of levirate marriage meant that if a man died before fathering sons—who would provide care and security for his wife—his brother had the duty to marry her and give her a son. The son born through this second brother would be considered not his but his brother's, however. Since Er was the firstborn, any son legally born to him would be the heir and could claim the firstborn's double share of inheritance.

This passage about Onan "spill[ing] his seed" (Genesis 38:9, AMP) isn't condemning masturbation but rather Onan's selfishness. He decided to take advantage of Tamar only for the pleasure of sex, without giving her the opportunity to become pregnant and receive security for her future. He is essentially treating her as a prostitute (ironic, right?), withholding her right to bear children and continue Er's family line. And by preventing Tamar from having children, Onan would inherit the double portion of the inheritance as the oldest surviving son.

We don't know if Onan's family knew he was unwilling to fulfill his duty to his wife and deceased brother, but God certainly did. Genesis 38 tells us God put Onan to death because his actions were wicked.

Poor Tamar. Two horrible husbands have now passed away, and Judah, her father-in-law, decides she must be cursed. And so, through continued inaction, Judah withholds yet another opportunity for her to have a child, reluctant to give her to his youngest son, Shelah. In other words, Judah would rather keep his youngest son "safe" than honor the deaths of his two older sons with the hope that Shelah's two oldest sons would continue their family name. Judah's fear or anger (or both!) would result in Er and Onan's family lines being severed from history.

With the excuse that Shelah was still too young for marriage, Judah makes it clear that Tamar is no longer welcome to live with his household. Hearing that news must have knocked the wind out of her. It was not typical for a wife to be sent home to her family, even as a widow. In her book on Tamar, Nigerian author, speaker, and architect Olajumoke Adenowo puts it beautifully:

> This was not the norm. Now she was part of the family, her place—irrespective of her circumstances—was supposed to be retained and secure. It was one thing to be ashamed, embarrassed, and by herself while in her new family. But to be told to pack her things and leave was unexpected. Where would she return to? There was a likelihood there was no room anymore for her in her parents' home. But since Judah, her father-in-law, had given the command, she had no choice.[15]

The years tarried on with no word. What began as a vindictive and selfish punishment for Tamar became more of an "out of sight, out of mind" topic for Judah. As time wore on, he probably didn't think about her much at all. Judah selfishly forgot he had placed Tamar's life in limbo, likely as an unwelcome servant for her own family.

Up until verse 12, when we learn that Judah's wife died, Tamar has played a passive role in the story. As Carolyn Custis James comments, "She was always the object of the action. Judah *got* her for Er, *gave* her to Onan, and *sent* her home to wait for Shelah."[16] Up until now, we don't have a shred of commentary from Tamar. We don't see her doing anything other than what she's told, in faith that the men charged with caring for her would do just that. She has accepted her fate after the death of two husbands and has carried the humiliation of being sent away. After so many years wearing the black garb of a widow and living in shame at her parents' home, waiting for Judah's third son to come of age, Tamar eventually realizes Shelah has grown old enough—yet no one has sent for her. The realization that they never would must have thundered through her like a storm.

And so, Carolyn Custis James says, "Now the verbs belong to her."[17] James continues,

> In a flurry of deliberate action, Tamar shed her widow's garments along with her passivity, veiled herself to play the prostitute and conceal her true identity, and placed herself in Judah's path. He has been without a wife for some time now. Tamar will exploit his loneliness.[18]

2. Okay, so let's talk about this. Considering what we know about how custom protects the family line, why do you think Tamar may have acted this way?

Historians of ancient Hittite and Assyrian law have discovered that the levirate practice extended to the father-in-law, as well. This aspect of the law was later banned, but it seems likely that in this time period, Tamar understood her rights: that because Shelah was not taking her hand and doing what is right (another not-great son, surprise, surprise), the next and only choice to fulfill the duty of giving her sons was Judah himself. And since Judah was a widower, she wouldn't be wronging his wife by her actions.[19]

Nowhere within Scripture does God say to simply sit on our hands and wait for things to fall into our laps. He asks us to trust, sure. But we are to move and act, right? James, the half brother of

Jesus,[20] talks about how faith is shown to be alive through works (James 2). Works don't give us salvation, but when we follow Him, God *asks us to show up*. If we love God, action is inevitable!

3. Where is God asking you to show up? Where might He be prodding you to move forward as part of His restorative work in the world?

_____

_____

_____

Tamar wasn't raised knowing anything about the God of Israel—and certainly she wouldn't have learned much about Him in Judah's household. It's obvious he didn't lead his family in the ways of God like his forefathers did. Even so, I wonder if she felt His presence in her loneliness. He was writing her into His story, after all. And she loved the same way Jesus loves, even toward those who don't deserve it. Yes, she was preserving her future, but she was doing it in a way that honored her first husband, Er. As evil as he was, she was fulfilling her duty to continue his family line.

After all those years in Judah's house, Tamar must have known his true character. It was clear he was not a godly man, despite his upbringing. She knew he would be easily enticed—and he was. Like a strong and determined businesswoman, Tamar exacted payment before service, and he quickly complied. When he fell asleep after the deed was done, she was able to slip away with his cord, staff, and signet ring (an official stamp that proved authenticity and position).

Later, reluctant to find this prostitute to exchange the promised goat for his personal items, Judah sent a friend, who came back with word that no prostitute was on the road to Enaim. (Which would make sense! Temple prostitutes wouldn't typically be on the road—they would be at the temple itself. Judah was *so* played.)

4. Three months later, Judah is told that Tamar is pregnant, and in a fury, he commands that she be burned. Stoning would have been the typical way for an unfaithful woman to die. Why do you think Judah responded with fire instead?

We don't know the reason for certain, but Judah was probably desperate to be rid of her. After two sons dropped dead after marrying Tamar, perhaps Judah thought *she* was the evil one, putting a curse on the family.

Imagine the scene: Tamar is condemned for being pregnant. Her enraged father-in-law demands she be burned to death. Verse 25 says she was "brought out," but I have to wonder what was happening behind that description. She was with child—a child she had been waiting for all these years. Surely those mama instincts had kicked in—there's no way she walked out of her own volition. Was she dragged by her hair or a flailing limb, screaming and clawing and scratching, holding on to anything that might keep her from her death sentence? She had to be desperate to protect the precious baby (actually, babies!) in her womb.

But frantic, flailing desperation is not what we see in what she does next.

5. How does Tamar announce the truth to Judah?

I'd be screaming, "The baby is yours!" and "I tricked you! It's me! I'm the fake temple prostitute!," a mixture of snot and tears muddling my face. But not our girl. Just as Nanye'hi was able to act decisively even in the face of her grief and terror, Tamar sees clearly what the next step is. And even in this horrific moment, she proves herself a woman of integrity. She doesn't name Judah or try to ruin his reputation. A Torah commentary authored by female rabbis notes that Tamar believes it is better to die than publicly humiliate someone and that "she does not report directly that Judah is the father; rather, she sets it up so that he confesses."[21]

6. Why do you think Tamar tells Judah in this way?

_____

_____

_____

Tamar gave Judah the chance to finally—*finally*—do the right thing. She made him face the tangible evidence of his own sin and then waited to see what he would choose to do. And possibly for the first time in his life, Judah faced his own dark side. He didn't try to skirt it or avoid it. He absolved her of any fault and took it all on himself. He brought honor to her and called *her* the righteous one. The Lord used this unwaveringly brave woman to change the trajectory of Judah's heart and character.

> Twice the narrator states what Judah's sons did was "wicked in the LORD's sight." Twice he tells us God acted decisively to stop their wickedness. What is more, the narrator records Judah's condemnation of himself when he confesses his wickedness before God. But there is no reproach for Tamar, no "What Tamar did was wicked in the LORD's sight." Instead, the heavens are strangely silent.
> . . . According to the Bible, Tamar was righteous. She sided with God and did the right thing.[22]

Judah's decision to own his sin and acknowledge Tamar's righteousness seems to have turned him back toward the God of his fathers. We don't know if he married Tamar. Likely not—verse 26 says "he did not know her intimately again" (Genesis 38:26, CSB). Some commentators believe once a son is born, the levirate agreement has been fulfilled. Either way, we *do* know Judah would have brought Tamar back into his household and cared for her as she raised their twin sons, Perez and Zerah.[23] Two sons taken away because of evil, and two given because of righteousness. Judah has a second chance to grow honorable sons who love the One True God.

At some point, it seems that Judah even leaves Canaan and returns to the community of his father's household. If we flip over a few chapters to Genesis 42–45, we learn that during a famine, Jacob sends his sons to find grain in Egypt. Judah plays a key role in this story—one that highlights the deeper change he's undergone.

Little do these brothers know, the one they trafficked into slavery had become Pharaoh's second-in-command. Pharaoh told Joseph, "You will be over my house, and all my people will obey your commands. Only I, as king, will be greater than you. . . . I am placing you over all the land of Egypt" (Genesis 41:40-41, CSB). When his brothers arrive in Egypt, *Joseph* is the one they have to ask for food. They don't recognize him, and Joseph pretends he doesn't know them—because he wants to test their character to see if they have changed. As part of the second test, Joseph threatens to imprison Benjamin (their father's other beloved child, also born to the late Rachel).

This is when Judah shows how much he's changed. Judah willingly offers his own life in his younger brother's place (Genesis 44:32-34). No more hiding. No more running. No more abdicating responsibility. At Judah's words, Joseph begins sobbing and reveals the truth of his identity.

7. What pain and struggles did Jacob's family (and Judah) face from the time Joseph was trafficked to Egypt? How did each of these things turn around after Judah admitted his fault in the situation with Tamar?

_____

_____

_____

_____

_____

I love how Olajumoke Adenowo talks about Tamar's journey from neglected to blessed:

> Tamar went into widowhood and into isolation. What she didn't know was that she needed that time away to be prepared for the place God had created for her. Those who mocked didn't know there was a vision God had of her long before time began, and now the word was about to be activated. Isolation comes before a blessing. You can't be blessed in a crowd. It usually doesn't happen that way. It is in the innermost chamber that God anoints. Far away from the crowd.[24]

We don't see Tamar again, except in the far distant records of genealogies, where her profound role in the people of God becomes clear.

8. Flip over to 1 Chronicles 2:1-15. How many sons did Judah have? Which sons carried on the lineage?

_____

_____

_____

9. How does this passage show us God's purposes in times of isolation and struggle? How do those seasons prepare us to pursue what is right?

God used Tamar for His Kingdom purposes, plain and simple: Judah's family line was saved, as was Tamar's. Judah turned his back from the rebellious Canaanite life and went home and lived life with God and his father and brothers, bringing Tamar and his twin sons to be cared for with love and honor. He righted old wrongs, protecting family rather than offering up the lives of others for self-preservation. And then, many thousands of years later, the authority of Judah's staff—the Savior of the world—was born among us, a descendant of Judah and Tamar.

All this because Tamar stepped out and was bold.

Tamar's story was a quest for justice. A quest to make right that which was wrong. Despite her unorthodox methods, she was a woman of integrity who risked her life to fulfill her duty to both herself and her family. But this brave woman didn't know the larger story: that her actions, and the children and grandchildren and great-grandchildren who would follow, would be part God's plan not just for her father-in-law's family—but for the world.

Your greatest contribution to the world may not be something you do but someone you raise.

God can do the same with us. He can use us for great purposes when we're willing to be bold and do what is right. Even when it's scary, even when we feel like we're putting everything on the line, even when everyone around us doubts, *He will move.* Let's be women who pursue what is right.

Live a life worthy of the calling *you* have received.

EPHESIANS 4:1, NIV, EMPHASIS MINE

Talk to the Lord about being a woman who is bold enough to do what is right—even when it seems scary or unorthodox—when you feel God's promptings. Remember, this is your calling—your story and no one else's. God may not have called other women to the same things He's calling you toward. Others may not always understand. Follow Him anyway.

Amen.

Rahab

A Woman Who Chooses Growth

WEEK 2 • *Day 1*

LISTEN
Place your phone over the QR code for this week's sacred song.

READ JOSHUA 1–2

In the movie *Encanto*, each member of the extraordinary Familia Madrigal has special enchanted gifting—well, all but Mirabel, who, because she lacks a magical gift, isn't valued or given a voice like the others are.

Yet who in the family ends up saving the day when no one else can? Mirabel. She didn't need magic. What she needed was what she already had: bravery, insight, wisdom, intuition, and a resolute determination to grow beyond the hard things.

I see some echoes of Rahab's story in that movie: She, too, was an underestimated and overlooked woman who chose to lean into growth and rebuilding when things fell apart. This can be your story too. The loss of your reputation, your marriage, your career, your finances isn't the end of the story. How others see you doesn't define your worth. Bouncing back may feel more like hitting the bottom and crawling back up, wounded yet breathing. And that's okay. No matter what you've been through, you can choose growth. You can choose to turn your face toward the days ahead. You can believe that God can redeem and restore. And you can rebuild—and the exciting thing is that often the second time around, the foundation is even more solid. Growth doesn't start from ground zero. Every piece of rubble is a part of rebuilding.

Rahab enters Scripture in the middle of the action. For forty years, news of the God of the Israelites had spread through towns, villages, cities, and kingdoms. Everyone had heard how this all-powerful God protected His people as they fled from Pharaoh, parting the waters

RAHAB: A WOMAN WHO CHOOSES GROWTH   •   49

and allowing the Israelites to walk on dry land. They heard tales of manna pouring from the sky, of water flowing from a rock. The stories claimed that this God physically resided with His people, displaying His presence as a pillar of smoke by day and a tower of fire by night. Travelers murmured of miracles and fallen kingdoms, and many wondered if the unbelievable stories were only fables. Those who knew they weren't felt deeply afraid. Yet despite all the stories, despite all those who had chosen to turn from idols and toward this mighty God, the hearts of everyone in Jericho had turned to stone. All lived in doubt and disbelief—except for one smart and shrewd woman named Rahab.

Okay, hold on for a minute. A smart and *shrewd* woman named Rahab? Yeesh. I don't know about you, but I completely balk and cringe at that word. Personally, my brain goes straight toward the word *shrew*, which means "woman of violent temper and speech."[1] But *shrew* and *shrewd* are not the same things (thanks, English language). If you looked up the word *shrewd*, you'd actually find descriptions like "clever," "intelligent," "having or showing sharp powers of judgment; astute."[2] So to recap: None of want to be a shrew. But we definitely want to be shrewd (like Rahab!).

1. Why was Rahab's reaction to the people of Israel so out of the norm? What do you think made her different?

_____

_____

_____

I wish I could see your response in those lines above because I'd love to know what you think made Rahab different from every other person within the walls of Jericho. Want to know my answer? Why *not* her?

Whether you've loved Jesus for forty years or forty minutes, I want you to remember something: We are *all* chosen. We are *all* appointed. God deliberately empowers men and women overlooked by culture, those who seem to be without a voice or are exploited, wounded, and feel abandoned. God doesn't call the qualified; He qualifies the called. It is by His strength that we can do bold, crazy-sounding things. Maybe we think our stories are too broken, too hard, or even too ordinary for God to use. But that isn't possible.

> Take a good look, friends, at who you were when you got called into this life. I don't see many of "the brightest and the best" among you, not many influential, not many from high-society families. Isn't it obvious that God deliberately chose men and women that the culture overlooks and exploits and abuses, chose these "nobodies" to expose the hollow pretensions of the "somebodies"? That makes it quite clear that none of you can get by with blowing your own horn before God. Everything that we have—right thinking and right living, a clean slate and a fresh start—comes from God by way of Jesus Christ. That's why we have the saying, "If you're going to blow a horn, blow a trumpet for God."
>
> 1 CORINTHIANS 1:27-31, MSG

To use the apostle Paul's observation, "Isn't it obvious that God . . . chose these 'nobodies'" to participate in His story of redemption? All we have to do is step forward (no matter how small that step feels).

2. What made Rahab someone who was ready to be used for God's purposes? Her name might give us a clue. Take a look at how it's translated in the BLB in Joshua 2:1. What are some meanings of this name?

Olajumoke Adenowo notes,

In ancient times, like in much of Africa and [Asia], people are named purposefully. Names can either be prophetic—what the parents or caregivers hope for, believe, and pray that the children become—or determined by the circumstances of their birth. . . .

Rahab, sometimes spelled Rachab, was given the name which when interpreted in the Hebrew language meant Expansion, Spaciousness, and Enlargement.[3]

And yet . . . these meanings are not how is Rahab generally remembered.

3. Flip to Hebrews 11:30-31. Coined *The Faith Hall of Fame*, this chapter names men and women who placed their trust in God, who in turn worked incredible things with their willing hearts. Rahab is one of them. Yet how is she described?

We have been so busy celebrating the mythical evangelical heroes that we've forgotten that heroes come in all walks of life, callings, and success ratios. God marks a hero very differently than the world does.[4]

SARAH BESSEY

4. Head to the BLB and pull up Hebrews 11:31. Tap on *Interlinear*, then scroll down until you see *pornē* (πόρνη, pronounced *por-nay*), a precursor to our English word *porn*. What do we learn here as this word is translated?

Pretty much what we expected, right? Whether she willingly stepped into this lifestyle or it was placed on her shoulders, Scripture is clear that prostitution was Rahab's past.

I know, I know: This isn't easy to talk about. But God works in the truth of our stories, not just in what we're comfortable with. We can't ignore that even Jesus' family history was full of brokenness and pain. Like in our families, things are often complicated.

5. Head back to your Bible and this time pull up James 2:25, the mention of Rahab in the New Testament. Why is this verse important not only for her but for us, as well?

The world needs more female truth tellers. It needs more women who not only have faith but also embody that faith. James reminds us that while our walk with Christ emerges from faith, our faith comes to life in how we interact with the world around us. We need to share it as we live it! Ancient cultures told and retold stories to friends, sons, daughters, and communities—and so should we. Let's be women who are bold enough to rise up and tell the truth about fellow women who have stepped out and stepped up. Bravery doesn't come without fear or obstacles. Bravery just means we stepped out anyway.

The shame of what Rahab had done was tacked on to her name, for all to see and judge. And yet? She is the one who saved her family. The one who believed, who lived. The prostitute becomes a root firmly planted into the family line of the Savior of the world. How often have we judged others, not realizing God may use them for something great?

Rahab: a woman of expansion and growth, or a harlot? How do we get out from under a name, whether given at birth or acquired by life?

6. Have you been given a name or label that didn't speak life into you? Or a title that only showed a fraction of who you are? How did you respond to that name?

Rahab may still be called a prostitute, even today. But that's not all she was. She didn't allow the label to define her. She chose to live a more spacious life. She chose to grow. The other day my friend Andi noted that if we don't grow, we're going to deteriorate, regress, and decay. This is why an ice cube melts: It is no longer working on freezing. This is why a tire goes flat, even when it hasn't been punctured. If a car or a bike sits unused, the tires will simply deflate over time.

It's the same for us. When we're not actively growing, or doing what we're purposed to do, we'll deflate. We'll get all soft and unusable. Growth is all about progression—if you want to be fulfilled, if you want to become someone who truly makes an impact, you must grow. Think about it: Your relationship with Christ or your spouse or friends, your muscles, your mind—all need to be used and strengthened or they will atrophy and break down.

When I think of this concept, my mind goes straight to working out. Do you know what muscle hypertrophy is? This is what happens when the fibers of muscles sustain damage or injury (through exercise). As the muscles are strained and damaged, the body jumps into repair mode, fusing them, which increases the mass and size of the muscles. In other words, the struggle enhances the growth.

This is why I think Scripture still refers to Rahab as a prostitute. It's God infusing fractured and damaged sections of our life together with His glory and His great purpose. We don't need to hide our cracks because the pouring in of the Holy Spirit has strengthened us to become women of greater strength and deep growth that we wouldn't have otherwise become.

7. In what ways has God grown you through brokenness in your own life? How has this strengthened your relationship with Christ?

_____

_____

_____

Rahab became a leader, a truth teller, a woman of virtue and faith. The name of her past was part of her story, but it wasn't the final chapter. And it doesn't have to be for you, either.

> Now when they saw the boldness of Peter and John, and perceived that they were *uneducated, common men,* they were astonished. And they recognized that they had been with Jesus.
>
> ACTS 4:13, EMPHASIS MINE

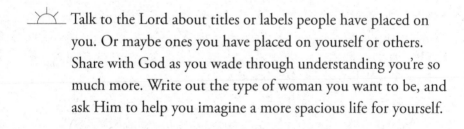 Talk to the Lord about titles or labels people have placed on you. Or maybe ones you have placed on yourself or others. Share with God as you wade through understanding you're so much more. Write out the type of woman you want to be, and ask Him to help you imagine a more spacious life for yourself.

_____

_____

_____

_____

_____

_____

_____

Amen.

WEEK 2 • *Day 2*

 LISTEN
Place your phone over the QR code for this week's sacred song.

 READ JOSHUA 2 *(in a different version than you read on day 1)*

In 1867, only a few years after the Emancipation Proclamation was signed, Sarah Breedlove was born on a Louisiana plantation—the same one, in fact, where her parents had been forced to work as enslaved people. That's where she began, but it's not where she remained. She later became known as Madam C. J. Walker, the first self-made female millionaire in US history. And not only that— she became a philanthropist, an advocate, and a change maker. In Madame Walker's own words,

> I am a woman who came from the cotton fields of the South. I was promoted from there to the washtub. Then I was promoted to the cook kitchen, and from there I promoted myself. . . . I have built my own factory on my own ground.[5]

Her life was far from easy. She was orphaned at the age of seven, married at fourteen, a mother at seventeen, and a widow at twenty. The world saw her as no more than an exhausted, poor, young widow with patchy hair as a result of a scalp ailment and hands perpetually wrinkled from hours working in soapy water. One day as she bent over the dishes, she realized that her body wouldn't allow her to do this work forever. She wanted more for her daughter's future, too, so she decided to make a dramatic change. After years of tenacity and intentional decisions, by 1905 she launched her own line of hair products for African American women: "Madam Walker's Wonderful Hair Grower."[6] Author Tanya Dalton observes,

In a time when most Black women were addressed by surname only or as *Auntie*, Madam Walker's new moniker was a signal of self-respect. Not only was she breaking the patterns of her past, she was breaking the patterns of society as well.[7]

Madam Walker refused to be defined by her label. With determination and intentionality, she grew beyond her difficult past. And today we'll discover the same was true for Rahab.

Rahab lived in the *and*. There wasn't one word to describe her. There isn't one way to describe you, either.

1. Circle all the words or phrases that remind you of . . . you!

outdoorsy	dreamer	book nerd	creative cook
clumsy	activist	lipstick lover	reliable
health-conscious	student	shy	extrovert
#girlboss	sports lover	girly	mom
teacher	messy bun wearer	tenacious	green thumb
organized	DIYer	grandmother	active
yoga pants lover	artsy	sensitive	sister
realist	leader	unorganized	strong
daughter	veggie lover	night owl	introvert
advocate	morning person	style trendsetter	car dancer

Look at the descriptions you circled. Do any seem to conflict? For example, some of mine are:

introvert and leader
lipstick lover and outdoorsy
shy and strong

The reality is, we are all women of *and*. None of us are just one thing. We are complex—because we are made in the image of a complex God who also lives in the *and*. As author Sarah Bessey notes, "He is both just and loving, the Lion and the Lamb. He is truth and grace."[8] And in the person of Jesus, God is both human and divine.

This is what's so great about living a life of *and*. You were created to lean into the multidimensional woman you are. Nobody should be pigeonholed—not you, not me, and certainly not Rahab.

2. Flip over to Proverbs 31:10-31 in your Bible. Or if you're already familiar with it, grab your phone or laptop and read it in a translation that's not quite as familiar. (One of my favorites—for times when I want the tone or essence of a passage—is the beautiful poetry of *The Message*.) How do you think Rahab's life might reflect aspects of this passage?

A lot of us have thought that this passage is telling us what a woman *should* be—an unrealistic, burdensome expectation. But this portion of Scripture isn't describing a real-life woman but rather the qualities and characteristics King Lemuel's mother hoped her son would find in a godly woman. Today in Jewish tradition, this proverb is read as a blessing over women—not a statement of what women *should* be but rather a recognition of the many good things women bring to the world.[9]

At this point in Rahab's story, she isn't married, nor does she have children. But if we look more closely at Joshua 2, I think we'll find that she exhibits many of the qualities from Proverbs 31. Why? Well, let's talk about business for a minute.

I mentioned briefly yesterday that Rahab likely didn't go into the life of prostitution as her number one career choice. Something devastatingly hard probably pushed her into the lifestyle, making her feel as if this was her only choice. What we do know, however, is that she was smart, clever, astute, and discerning.

3. In what ways was she these things? Read Joshua 2 again if you need a little refresher.

smart:

clever:

astute:

discerning:

Out of all the people in Jericho, Rahab was the one who both knew these men were spies and realized it was wise to protect them. How did she know they were spies? Everyone in Jericho knew that the Israelites were encamped across the river and that an attack was imminent. But Rahab believed the stories about this powerful God they served. Perhaps she knew the legend of the spies Moses had sent forty years prior. Twelve spies had entered the Promised Land, and all but two had reported back that taking it was an impossible feat. Because of this, an exodus that should have taken eleven days ended up taking forty years. It wasn't that they didn't know *how* to get to the land of milk and honey . . . it was that because of their lack of faith, God had removed their permission to enter. Joshua and Caleb (the two spies who trusted God and believed God would accomplish what He had promised) were the only men still alive when God gave them the green light. The rest of the entire generation of men and women who came out of Egypt had been buried. This new generation would receive the land that had been promised all those years before.

Now the Israelites were back. Would spies be sent again? I have a feeling Rahab thought they would—and because her home was set into the towering wall of this great city, she was keeping watch through her window.

With the Lord on her side, a woman of discernment sees what's really going on. Rahab saw the spies. She believed in the power of the God they served. And she knew that keeping them safe was her best chance of keeping her family safe as well.

A detail we often skim over in this story is how Rahab hid these men. When you read about Rahab hiding the men under stalks of flax, really think about that for a moment. How much of the stuff must she have had on her roof to ensure these men were covered completely? Think of the sheer volume! Bushels piled high, enough to obscure the obvious shape of two grown men. This isn't something she would have just happened to have lying around. Acquiring that much flax takes effort and intentionality. Why did she have such a massive amount, anyway?

A few years ago, I came upon a book that completely changed the way I looked at our girl Rahab. As Gene A. Getz wrote about Joshua,[10] he theorized that Rahab didn't have this much flax on her roof by accident. What if it was there for a purpose? What if "Rahab the prostitute" was living into her true name, growing out of the dark place life had put her and moving into something more?

Scratching your head? Let's explore this a bit.

First, a bit about flax. The milk I poured into my latte this morning is made from it, as are the seeds I sprinkle into my cashew yogurt with some fresh berries. Flax is full of omega-3s and fiber and is a high source of lignans (which by the way, lowers the risk of cancer). In Rahab's time, though, flax was used for two things: It was pressed and heated to produce linseed oil; or it was pounded until the fine fibers were separated, used to create a thread or yarn, and spun into linen.[11]

4. Why do you think Rahab had flax?

Maybe Rahab wasn't physically toiling in the sun, plowing or pulling the four-foot-tall, blue-flowered stalks straight from the ground (but who knows, maybe she was). Perhaps she purchased the bundles of flax stems. Either way, though, flax was on her roof—a lot of it.

After dipping flax in water, people put it on the roof to dry, which was only one step in a long process of turning the stalks into textiles. After retting (soaking the flax in water to soften the woody dressing) and drying the flax stalks, someone would break, scrunch, and heckle the flax to make it usable—and after all that, you're on your way to having yarn or thread! Whew! That's a lot.

So let's look back at Rahab. The only reason she would have had flax on her roof in this time was to make textiles—intense, backbreaking, tedious work.

5. Given what we know now about this aspect of Rahab's life, do you think the label "Rahab the prostitute" was one that applied to her in her present—or just in her past? Why or why not?

Crazy, right? Of course we can't say for sure, but when we really dig into the historical context, it seems plausible that Rahab had chosen to step beyond her life of prostitution, to grow instead into a businesswoman who made linen textiles. And it was this growth—along with her growth in spiritual sensitivity—that equipped her to serve God in hiding His people.

But there's even more to this, if we dig into the context of *what* she was making. Flip your Bible over to Ezekiel 44:17-19. (*The Message* shares this passage especially beautifully if you're able to hop online and read it in this translation!)

6. What kind of fabric was to be worn in the Temple? What do you think this has to do with Rahab?

 ## *History Lesson*

Linen is one of the oldest developed textiles, dating back around ten thousand years ago. Flax was one of the first crops to be cultivated, and from that, linen became one of the oldest-developed textiles. Linen artifacts from the Dead Sea area have been found dating as far back as 6000 BC.[12]

The Babylonians are thought to have started weaving flax first, but the Egyptians made linen famous in the ancient world. Some linen was woven so finely, it was completely sheer. (The finer the linen, the wealthier you were. Pharaoh and his family wore the finest and thinnest.) Thanks to the dry Egyptian climate, archaeologists have found remarkably well-preserved linen in tombs—not just the linen strips wrapping each mummy, but linen dresses, tunics, and bolts of linen cloth (especially beautiful ones from King Tut's tomb!).

In an article on biblical references to linen and flax seed, Deborah Greenhill wrote,

Flax was so important to Egypt during the time of
Moses, that the Bible records its destruction during
the plague of hail, along with other essential crops.
The flax was in its full, ready-to-harvest boll (bud)
stage when the plague of hail struck (Exodus Chapter 9). This must have been financially devastating
to the farmers who had worked hard, waiting for a
harvest.[13]

Why am I taking the time to tell you all this? Stay with me . . . I
really do have a point. Flip over to Exodus 35, where Moses asks the
people of Israel to help build the Tabernacle:

5-9Gather from among you an offering for GOD. Receive on
GOD's behalf what everyone is willing to give as an offering:
gold, silver, bronze; blue, purple, and scarlet material; *fine
linen*; goats' hair; tanned rams' skins; dolphin skins; acacia
wood; lamp oil; spices for anointing oils and for fragrant
incense; onyx stones and other stones for setting in the
Ephod and the Breastpiece.
    10Come—all of you who have skills—come and make
everything that GOD has commanded.
EXODUS 35:5-10, MSG, EMPHASIS MINE

How exciting to create something tangible for the Lord! Scripture
tells us hearts were moved and spirits stirred as His people jumped
into action. Then, in Exodus 35:25 (I particularly like how the ESV
puts it), we read this:

And every _____ _____ spun with her
hands, and they all brought what they had spun in blue and
purple and scarlet yarns and fine twined linen.

7. What two words are missing? Let's head over to the BLB and dig in further. Look up this verse and tap into the *Interlinear* section, so we can see what *ḥāḵām* (חָכָם; pronounced *hah-kahm*) means. Write down various words given that stand out to you:

_____

_____

_____

"Skillful," "prudent," "wise (ethically and religiously)."[14] Huh. I understand *skillful*, but *wise*? If we scroll down further to the *Gesenius' Hebrew-Chaldee Lexicon*, we see that *wise-hearted* is often a better word to translate *ḥāḵām* (חָכָם).[15]

So if we were to translate this verse from Hebrew word-for-word, it might say something like this:

> And all the women who were wise-hearted with their hands spun and brought that which they had spun—of blue and of purple, of scarlet and of fine linen.

We can see why our English Bibles word things a little differently, right? The grammar isn't great, and it's a tad confusing. But this might get us a little closer to what the writer of Exodus was getting at.

These weren't just women who were good at weaving. Their participation in this work wasn't just about getting a job done. They brought *wise hearts* with them. These women were drawn to deeper things, were motivated to bring what they had as an offering to God.

That sounds a little bit like what we're learning about Rahab, doesn't it? There was so much more to her than met the eye—and she offered all the considerable skills and insights at her disposal to serve the God of Israel.

We read earlier that people (typically priests) were allowed to enter the presence of God only if they were wearing clothing made of linen. Rahab likely had no idea that her daily work was actually a holy assignment given to wise-hearted women among God's people, but God was preparing her to be one of His own.

8. How might God want to meet you in the midst of your daily tasks? How might He be preparing you in the middle of your everyday work?

_____

_____

_____

_____

What if Rahab hadn't collected the flax? Where would the men have hidden? God honors our work, even the things that seem boring or arduous. He's always writing a bigger story.

As you go through your day-to-day responsibilities, pay attention to what God is forming within you and what He's inviting you into. He wants to use you exactly where you are. Maybe you can take stress off your roommate by cooking dinner for her as she studies for an exam. Perhaps you love your husband by picking up his shirts from the cleaners. Maybe you can have a fun treat waiting on the counter after school for your kids to munch on as they do homework. Bring joy to your elderly neighbor by making her a meal or decorating her home for a holiday. Shovel the snow off the driveway of a single mom you know. Bring a hot chocolate over to the person shivering with the sign on the corner.

Sometimes things don't feel large to the person giving, but they're immense to the one receiving. Step into that larger story by allowing God to use your simple offerings in another's life today.

9. Write down some ideas of how God can use your everyday gifts:

_____

_____

_____

_____

In the same way, let your light shine before others, so that they may see your good works and give glory to your Father who is in heaven.

MATTHEW 5:16

Talk to the Lord about living a life full of *ands* . . . and how He wants to meet you in the midst of your day-to-day tasks.

_____

_____

_____

_____

_____

_____

_____

_____

_____

_____

Amen.

WEEK 2 • *Day 3*

LISTEN
Place your phone over the QR code for this week's sacred song.

READ JOSHUA 2 *in a different version than day 1 or day 2. (Yes, really. We notice different things in the text when it's written differently!)*

When our kids were young, Ben worked for a company that whisked the sales team (and their spouses . . . score!) away to a five-star resort—typically somewhere over-the-top on the beaches of Hawaii or Mexico—for a week every year for "meetings." We'd enjoy spa days, live bands, sailing adventures, and a wedding-reception-worthy dinner party each evening (and yes, I recognize how insanely privileged this is!). We don't have family in-state, so it was always an extra big deal to be able to go—we'd have to fly family in (typically my mom) to care for our kids while we were gone.

One year I was particularly exhausted and overwhelmed and didn't have the chance to shop for a new dress for the extravagant final dinner of the trip. (This was the kind of thing where mama needed to get seriously dressed up.) Thankfully, I had a great dress in the back of my closet, and it still fit. It may not have been the latest style or brand-new, but that wasn't a big deal—it felt great on (and, *hello*, it had *pockets*).

But as I pulled the dress out of my closet to fold up and place into my suitcase just before the trip, I saw it.

A stain. Right there on the stomach of the pristine white dress.

And I could *not* get it out.

Knowing there was no way I had time to go shopping with six little kids in tow, I decided the DIYer in me needed to show up. *Dye it!* I thought. I had some red fabric dye from who-knows-what project. And this would be a great teachable moment for my kids, right? *Let's all be together in the kitchen and watch Mommy turn this disappointment around!*

It'll be fiiiiine, I convinced myself.

Was it fine? No. No, it was not. Not even kind of. Did the dye work? I mean . . . technically? Sure, the dress wasn't white anymore, but it was definitely far from red. How much red pigment do you need to dye a cocktail dress? Answer: *more than I had*. This fun-sounding DIY-teachable moment ended up with a horribly ugly, disastrous, and *so*-not-wearable dress (sob).

Apparently, you need *a whole lot* of red dye for something to turn red. It wasn't even a cute pink. The rest of the day, my kids kept pointing out other red things around the house, talking about what a massive amount of dye it took to create it. (Salt in the wound.)

Moral of the story? (Other than: Make sure your important outfit is okay more than a day or so before a trip.) When Joshua 2 talks about Rahab tying a red cord in her window, she would have had to use a *whole lot of dye*. So when I talk about Rahab possibly overseeing a booming textile business? This red cord is the other reason I believe this to be true.

As Gene A. Getz explains in his book *Joshua: Living as a Consistent Role Model,*

> The "scarlet rope" or "thread"—even more than the flax—points to a change of profession. When the ancients made dye, they would boil it out of rocks. And since liquid dye was difficult to transport and store, they would put a piece of rope into the dye to absorb it. Cloth makers then would buy pieces of the rope to dye their clothes. While the cloth was boiling in water, they would drop a piece of the dyed rope in the container and the color would transfer from the rope to the fabric. Usually a very small piece of rope—six inches or so—would dye a large quantity of cloth. . . .

Rahab had enough red rope accumulated to hang it all the way over a wall that may have been as high as thirty feet. For a clothmaker, that's a lot of rope! Evidently Rahab's cloth business was no minor operation.[16]

Rahab had enough red rope that she could tie it and hang it out of her window. We're not talking a tiny amount here. It would have been visible to anyone looking at the city.

The day Rahab hid the spies and tied the cord out her window was her first moment of active faith. Just as she had stretched beyond the brokenness that had defined her, she now stretched out toward the God of Israel. As her trust in God grew, so did her willingness to step out of what was expected. She was ready to move, and God was ready to use her. Taking her out of a life of wounding, He bound her up—and, like the blood of Jesus that would one day be poured out, her red rope spilled from her window in acknowledgment of the promise of salvation.

So why am I focusing so much on this red cord? Because I suspect it has a lot more to tell us about Rahab's story.

1. Let's head to the BLB. Click on Joshua 2:15 and get into the *Interlinear* section. Scroll down to the word *rope* or *ḥēḇel* (חֶבֶל, pronounced *heh-bel*). What does this word mean?

Cord, rope, line . . . sure, makes sense. Mind not blown here, right? *But wait, there's more!* I know you've read this story several times by now, but I'm going to ask you to read verses 15-21 again anyway. Don't be annoyed—seriously, do it. Something odd is happening here.

2. Give me an order of events in these several verses:

_____

_____

_____

_____

_____

Okay, so she lets them down by a rope (חֶבֶל, *ḥēḇel*) . . . and *then* she has a conversation with them about hiding out for three days? And after *that*, they tell her to "tie this scarlet cord in the window through which you let us down" (Joshua 2:18)?

So either they're yelling back up from the ground, or more likely, they're speaking really quickly as Rahab is letting them down. The reason this is significant is that one of the men says, "tie this scarlet cord." *This* scarlet cord. As in the one he has in his hands that she's letting him down with.

I always visualized that scarlet cord as a little curtain-tie being shown in the window. You know, like a decorative feature. But no! As Getz explained previously, this would have been a crazy-long rope, eventually intended to dye a massive amount of cloth.

Let's keep digging.

3. Look at Joshua 2:18. What word is used for *cord* here? Now go to Joshua 2:21. What is it there?

_____

Remember, *ḥēḇel* (חֶבֶל) was the term used in verse 15. Joshua 2:18 and 2:21 use the word *tiqvâ* (תִּקְוָה, pronounced *tik-vah*). So why the two different Hebrew terms for the word *cord* in such a short space?

I wanted to make sure I was really getting this, so I asked a Jewish friend of mine. She said, "Yes! Both these words mean the same thing. They wouldn't necessarily mean two different ropes. The terms could be used interchangeably."

4. Look back at *tiqvâ* in the BLB. What is the second meaning of the word? How do you think that plays into this story?

_____

_____

When I asked her about *tiqvâ*, she said, "It means hope and expectation. It doesn't mean rope." And then she texted back a minute later: "But it does mean 'to tie a rope,' though. It's an action word."

Here comes the big light bulb!

Rahab let the spies down and down and *actively tied hope and expectation into her window with the rope!* Can you hear me yelling? Because I'm seriously yelling this.

Nineteenth-century author and Bible teacher William Evans once said, "The atonement is the scarlet cord running through every page in the entire Bible. Cut the Bible anywhere, and it bleeds."[17] Rahab's growth—reaching out of her life of prostitution, moving toward the God who would save her and her family—was an expansion toward redemption. She was living into her name. She was again stepping out toward a fresh start, but this time through the love of a God whose atonement is, as Evans wrote, "red with redemption truth."[18] Rahab had no idea this red cord acted as foreshadowing of the Messiah, the One who came for everyone, no matter their history or heritage. She had no way of recognizing she was changing history, no way of knowing the walls around her would tumble. All she knew was she'd rather have a life of uncertainty with Him than one of certainty within the walls that had been built around her.

5. Flip your Bible over to Matthew 7:24-25. How do these verses apply to Rahab's story?

Inside the towering walls of Jericho, Rahab's house was built upon the only rock that could save her. She may have been surrounded by tons of rocks, but because she built her תִּקְוָה *tiqvâ*—her hope and expectation—upon the Rock of Ages, she and all her family were saved.

As women who love the Lord our God, we put our תִּקְוָה *tiqvâ* in Him, the Everlasting Rock. And when we do, He saves us. Over and over and over, He saves us. The red cord was Rahab's Passover blood. The angel of death passed right over her.†

Rahab was a woman of growth because she could see outside the larger picture. She may not have known the details, but she knew life had to be bigger than her current situation. She could have pleaded to go with the spies, to escape that very night from the destruction that would befall her city. Yet she stayed. Resolute, she actively lived in hope and expectation because she believed in a big God whom she had only heard stories about.

6. Where in your life do you need to live in hope and expectation of what God can do?

---

† There is so much to dig into through Rahab's story. If you'd love to learn more, I encourage you to check out my seven-week study in the book of Joshua, *Leading Wherever You Are.*

Hope can't exist unless we actively tie our expectations of growth around prayer and possibility. When we choose to see beyond our current situation, to dare to dream of what God has ahead of us, we can become women of expansion rather than women of dissatisfaction. Like Rahab, we can set our sights on the One who ignores labels and invites us into His bigger story.

You will feel secure, because there is hope [תִּקְוָה *tiqvâ*];
   you will look around and take your rest in security.

JOB 11:18

Talk to the Lord about something in your life that feels daunting right now. Ask Him to help you become a woman of expansion, to live full of active hope and expectation even in the face of fear.

Amen.

Ruth

A Woman Who Loves Radically

WEEK 3 • *Day 1*

LISTEN
Place your phone over the QR code for this week's sacred song.

READ RUTH 1

Four of our children are adopted, and that comes with heartache. The thing is, people often like to put adoption in a pretty little box. We've heard stuff like "They must be so thankful to have you" and "It's so great you saved them!" (ugh). The reality is, although our story *is* beautiful, it's also full of significant loss. One of my daughters cries for her "Ethiopia Mommy" every single day. Every *day*! No matter how much we laugh and love in our family, my children carry stories filled with deep, deep pain (and no, we certainly didn't "save" them).

Sadly, that's life. But why is it we so often romanticize hard stuff? Is it that we can't handle the pain-filled truth that life is difficult? Trying to turn something into a pretty picture undervalues the beauty in the struggle. It causes us to miss the richness and redemption of love.

So let's talk about the book of Ruth. Because I think we tend to do the same kind of thing to this story. A note in the Bible currently in front of me says that "the book of Ruth is a delightful short story with a classical plot that moves from crisis to complication to resolution . . . inviting us to identify with [characters'] personal anxieties and joys and in the end to celebrate the movement from emptiness and frustration to fulfillment and joy."[1]

I don't know about you, but that doesn't feel like it really captures what's happening here. Ruth's life is *hard*. Her husband is dead. The other two men in her husband's family, her brother-in-law and her father-in-law, are also dead. This means she's lost all her protection and security in a world that—as we know already—was not kind to women. As you read her story, think about what she might have been feeling. Think about the temptation to despair, the fear of starvation, the grief of loss.

The book of Ruth isn't a sweet love story plopped down to add some levity between the heaviness of Judges and 1 Samuel. The real human cost in this story is heavy. This isn't *Pride and Prejudice*, and Boaz is not Mr. Darcy.

Okay, so the delightful love-story angle is out. What's a better lens through which to read this story?

My background is in art history, which is why I find myself bringing some of the same questions to the Bible that I did to art:

- What was happening in the artist's town or country?
- What was happening culturally and politically?
- What social and economic factors do I need to learn about?

What was happening in the artist's personal life would help me understand what inspired the creation of a sculpture, painting, or even a song or poem. When studying the Bible, I ask myself similar things—but instead of focusing on the whys of the *artist*, I hone in on why *God* decided to include this in the pages of Scripture. Why this story? Why these people?

1. With our background questions in mind, let's go back to Ruth 1:1. What three things do we learn?

    1. _____

    2. _____

    3. _____

The first two pieces of information shed some light on the third.

2. What do we know about the time of the judges? (See Judges 2:6-23.)

During this time, God's chosen people wouldn't just up and move to Moab voluntarily. Moab was somewhere you passed through, not somewhere Israelites put down roots. What's more, this was an infamously dark time in Israel's history. We learn in Judges 17:6 and 21:25 that "everyone did what was right in his own eyes." When God gave His people judges, the Israelites would repent and turn back to God, but every time a judge died, the Israelites again chose evil. There was massive political unrest and government collapse. Horrific judgments befell Israel as they turned their backs on God again and again.

3. What do you think a move to Moab during the famine may have signified about Elimelech and Naomi's situation? What do you think convinced them to leave everything and go?

 History Lesson

If you do not drive out the inhabitants of the land from before you, then those of them whom you let remain shall be as barbs in your eyes and thorns in your sides, and they shall trouble you in the land where you dwell.

NUMBERS 33:55

RUTH: A WOMAN WHO LOVES RADICALLY • 77

God commanded the Israelites to drive out the Canaanites from the Promised Land, but they didn't kick everyone out as He commanded. The Moabites were an example of this. We don't know the full reasoning behind Israel's decision to keep these particular people around, but it may have been because of their partial family ties. Moab was the son of Abraham's nephew, Lot—the product of an incestuous encounter between an inebriated Lot and his daughter, who took advantage of her father to get pregnant. (Bleh.)

Why did a loving God command these groups and kingdoms to be slaughtered and driven out? Because God wanted His people to be set apart, holy, distinctly different from the evil nations around them. Both Leviticus and Deuteronomy share lurid details of Canaanite practices, including child sacrifice, worship of demonic idols, "sacred prostitution," and other vulgar (and often public) sexual acts. God makes it clear in that He is not giving Israel the land of milk and honey because of the people's righteousness or integrity but rather "because of the vile wickedness of these nations . . . GOD, your God, is dispossessing them before you so that he can keep his promised word to your ancestors" (Deuteronomy 9:5, MSG). God didn't want Israel to be seduced by the evil practices and idolatrous cultures of the Canaanites.

Was this move an example of Elimelech's lack of faith? This is what's generally recognized and taught. But I want to take it one step off the beaten path: The Bible doesn't tell us how they made their decision, and of course it's possible that Elimelech did not trust that God would protect their family and so took matters into his own hands. But wouldn't it be like God to ask Elimelech and his family to do something big and crazy sounding? It wouldn't have been the first time God had led his people to a strange land (look back at

Abraham's story!), nor was it the last. Shortly after the magi headed home after their visit with Jesus, an angel visited Joseph in a dream, saying, "Rise, take the child and his mother, and flee to Egypt, and remain there until I tell you, for Herod is about to search for the child, to destroy him" (Matthew 2:13).

Regardless of why Elimelech and Naomi moved, God was going to use their new home and new neighbors. He was about to write Ruth into His story. Maybe they needed to move so He could move.

But still, remember—this isn't a "meet cute" love story, where Elimelech and Naomi's son finds himself in an unfamiliar land only to meet the love of his life. No—Ruth's life became entwined with tragedy. And even if God had clearly led Elimelech and Naomi to Moab, Naomi was certainly questioning everything now.

4. Head over to 1:20 and write it down:

_____

_____

_____

Naomi proclaims that her new name is Mara (מָרָה, *bitter*). For many years I was taught that Naomi was just a grumpy ol' pessimist. A narcissistic, bitter mother-in-law who needs everything to be about her.

If you were taught that too, I'm sorry. Because we were taught wrong.

Naomi isn't a complainer. She isn't overly dramatic. We don't need her to calm down.

Think about what she has gone through and consider how realistic her state of mind is in the fallout. She is deeply steeped in depression and is incredibly open about it. No false self. No pretending everything's fine. Naomi's grief and anger at God are debilitating.

Naomi's heartache may have become full-blown anguish after the death of her husband and sons, but her sorrow probably began years prior, during the famine in Bethlehem that threatened their lives. I have several friends who are refugees from Sierra Leone and Sudan, and the ache, pain, and loss they've experienced are excruciating. The impact of famine is horrific, cascading into all sorts of terror and trauma.

This famine threatened Naomi's family's lives. They had likely gone hungry for a long time. She would have watched her beloved sons suffer. And the only way out was to move to a land that was often at war against her people. She was completely uprooted from everything she'd ever known, and she was likely shunned—or at least not wholly embraced—by the Moabites, those ancient enemies of Israel. That's a lot. But there's more.

We don't know much about Naomi's sons, Mahlon and Chilion, but let's head to the BLB and discover what their names mean.

5. Tap on the BLB app and head to Ruth 1:2. Once there, tap on the verse and then on *Interlinear*. Scroll down to first Mahlon's name and then Chilion's. Write what their names mean in the spaces below. (Go all the way down to *Gesenius' Hebrew-Chaldee Lexicon* if needed.)

Mahlon:

_____

_____

Chilion:

_____

_____

That's kind of telling, isn't it? We know nothing of Elimelech's death, but the passing of Naomi's boys might not have been super sudden. Remember, names during these days were given intentionally, imbued with significance. Giving her sons names like *sick* and *wasting away* wouldn't have been accidental. Naomi likely had many years of wringing her hands and dropping to her knees in prayer over the health of her precious children.

Watching your children in pain is agony. As I type this, one of our kids is going through some stuff so big and painful, I just can't wrap my mind around it. I think they expect God (and us) to give up on them, but we never will. But wow—does it hurt.

6. What pain are you carrying? Are there ways in which you can relate to Naomi? Why or why not?

Ruth's story begins with another woman's massive pain and loss. Naomi has lost everything—her land, her husband, her sons, her home. Ruth and her sister-in-law were both married for a decade, and neither had children. Naomi's family line had come to an end. This was it. Life as she knew it was over. With no male family member to provide food, shelter, and safety, she was doomed to become destitute. She's an outsider in a foreign country. And things in her own country were dark and painful. All this stress heaped high on top of her deep grief.

Naomi was a female Job.

Or, as Carolyn Custis James says, "I think Naomi actually out-Jobed Job."[2]

Think about it. Both Naomi and Job suffered the loss of a life they spent years creating and caring for. They both endured massive tragedy in the death of their family members. And yet Job still had his wife and friends by his side (not that they were helpful and encouraging, but still). And also? Job was not a woman (with no rights) and an immigrant (which equaled major second-class status).

Blow after blow became too much for Naomi.

It was too much. Just. Too. Much.

The woman is grieving. She's barely surviving, and she's done. D-O-N-E and undone. There's nothing left for Naomi in Moab, so she's going home, though she's been gone for years and doesn't have an actual home to go home to. Would her community embrace her? Would they even remember her?

Yet what does Ruth do?

Ruth, too, has lost everything. Her husband. The hope of children. But Ruth perhaps would have had a home to go back to. She could have started over right where she was. She was, after all, among her people in Moab. At the very least, she wasn't an outsider.

But Ruth does something extraordinary. She walks alongside. She goes with. She loves radically.

Radical love is at the heart of the gospel. Speaker and activist Lisa Sharon Harper shares that the writers of Matthew, Mark, Luke, and John not only "cared about an individual's reconciliation with God, self, and their communities," but "also focused on systemic justice, peace between people groups, and freedom for the oppressed."[3] This is our first glimpse of God's *why* in Ruth. He uses the unexpected, the marginalized, the outsider, to point the way toward the radical love of His reconciliation.

The heart of the gospel starts generations before the birth of Christ, hundreds of years before Jesus stepped into our human world with radical love to reconcile us to God. Ruth shows us this movement in action, the unflinching resolve to walk alongside a broken woman, to love big and love hard. Ruth cared about her mother-in-law and advocated with strength.

We criticize Orpah for turning home and not continuing the journey with Ruth and Naomi, but we shouldn't. It was the sensible decision. Naomi had nothing to give, nothing to ensure her own safety or bright future, much less someone else's. Ruth, too, should have bid Naomi good-bye and good luck. But she didn't. She chose to risk her own future and safety to care for the deeply wounded person in front of her. As the saying goes, love is a verb, an action. And because of that, radical love can seem crazy. It's an action full of sacrifice, with no guaranteed outcome. Ruth acts with revolutionary confidence and strength. It's as if she knew there was no other way.

Ruth shows us a glimpse of what Jesus ultimately showed us: that as we act in radical love, as we move toward the broken, we participate in the restoration of all things.

> Where you go, I go; and where you live, I'll live. Your people are my people, your God is my god; where you die, I'll die, and that's where I'll be buried, so help me GOD—not even death itself is going to come between us!
>
> RUTH 1:16-17, MSG

Talk to the Lord about being brave enough to love radically. Pour your heart out to Him as you ponder what it might mean to participate in His restoration of the brokenness around you.

Amen.

WEEK 3 • *Day 2*

LISTEN
Place your phone over the QR code for this week's sacred song.

READ RUTH 2

Back in 2019, Alex Borstein won an Emmy for Outstanding Supporting Actress in a Comedy Series (for *The Marvelous Mrs. Maisel*). I remember because her speech was so powerful. While accepting the award, she honored her grandmother's miraculous escape from death during the Holocaust:

> I want to dedicate this to the strength of a woman. . . . My grandmother turned to a guard. She was in line to be shot into a pit, and she said, "What happens if I step out of line?" And he said, "I don't have the heart to shoot you, but somebody will," and she stepped out of line. And for that, I am here, and for that my children are here. So, step out of line, ladies. Step out of line![4]

What a powerful question. What happens if I step out of line? What happens if I stand against this terrifying thing, if I look pain and despair in the face—and I decide to step out of line? I'm reminded of something Cleveland Cavaliers player Kevin Love posted on Instagram in support of gymnast Simone Biles: "Don't deny your story—defy the ending."[5]

Defy the ending.

Ruth and Naomi were in the middle of a hard story. Naomi didn't deny it or avoid it. She named exactly what she was going through. And Ruth doesn't tell Naomi to "get over it" or to "move on." She doesn't say anything trite, like "It could always be worse." No. Ruth chooses to support Naomi and stand with her. She comes up with a plan to take care of her mother-in-law, and she steps out of the line of expectation and culture. Ruth decides she will not accept hard as the end of her story.

Ruth couldn't do anything about the story she'd been handed, but she didn't give up either. Ruth defied the ending, and God will use her and Naomi's story for millennia to remind us all that the marginalized aren't disposable. As Carolyn Custis James notes, Ruth proved that "God does not have a separate definition for widows or a footnote outlining an image bearer hierarchy, where the widow drops to the bottom. According to God's definition, she is right up there with everyone else."[6] In God's economy, our struggle isn't what defines us. And, as Ruth shows us, radical love is what helps us defy the ending.

A quick side note before diving into the text: Today we meet Boaz, but he doesn't take over the story. He doesn't take the lead. This is significant. The book of Ruth breaks all the rules, highlighting two marginalized women with no voice. And instead of presenting them as weak and helpless, these women take command of the story line. They remain the main characters, and the men around them supply the supporting roles.

Before we get to Boaz, let's look at what our girls Naomi and Ruth are up to. With Naomi's blessing, off Ruth goes to gather fallen grain. We don't know why she goes to the fields alone. Perhaps Naomi is too old for hard labor. We know Naomi (er, Mara) continues to struggle with grief and depression, so maybe her despair is so debilitating that she can't get out of bed.

1. In verse 1 of this second chapter, we are told Naomi has a relative on her husband's side named Boaz. The narrator lets us in on this little tidbit of information, but Naomi doesn't mention it to Ruth. Why do you think she didn't mention Boaz before Ruth set out to find a field to glean?

Naomi's family has been gone for many years. Perhaps she didn't realize that Boaz was now a man of wealth and prominence. Or maybe Naomi doesn't know he's still alive, or she has forgotten about him. Or perhaps she's too steeped in depression for it to even occur to her to mention the man.

All that changes when, after a single day of work in the fields, Ruth arrives home with an ephah of barley, as well as lunch leftovers. It's only when Ruth shares about her day that Naomi mentions Boaz's relation to their family.

2. Flip to verses 5-12. In a nutshell, what's happening here?

_____

_____

_____

_____

3. It's obvious Boaz knew of Naomi's situation before his servant mentioned it in verse 6 (see verse 11). So why do you think this family member—a man who is presented to us as honorable and upright—has not reached out to Naomi?

_____

_____

_____

If we were to look in the BLB at Ruth 2:20 and dig into what Scripture says about Boaz being family, we'll learn that the word used is qārôḇ (קָרוֹב, pronounced kah-robe), which means: "neighbour," "kinsfolk, kinsmen," "allied," "near" (as in physically near, or as in "relationship and affinity"), "intimate acquaintance."[7]

Now, notice what this word doesn't mean—we don't get definitions like "brother, uncle, nephew, cousin," or anything that links him straight into Elimelech's immediate family line. So what kind of relative is he?

I suspect we're missing some cultural context here. I used to get so confused when my Asian and African friends would talk about their families. ("Hold on, Ester. Rachelle is your cousin? But your mom said she's not from her side and she looks nothing like your dad. I don't get it. Explain.") Many of my friends from other countries consider their good friends to be family because they share roots as a tribe or nation. The same is likely true here. So, to be clear: Boaz isn't ignoring family; he's likely from the same tribe as Elimelech, a distant friend of Naomi's late husband.

Verse 17 tells us Ruth gathered (and beat out) what resulted in an *ephah* (or about twenty dry quarts).[8] We might skip quickly past that piece of information, but let's pause for a moment to think about what that means. Twenty dry quarts would be approximately twenty-five pounds of barley.[9] And . . . that's a lot when you consider a couple things:

- Ruth worked behind the harvesters, gathering anything left behind or dropped. One by one, she'd pick up sheaf after sheaf (not bunches, like the harvesters in front of her). What a painstakingly slow and exhausting job. Her hands must have bled from picking the dry wheat-like stalks.

- Ruth's haul compares very favorably to the average compensation of paid field laborers in her day. Carolyn Custis James explains: "Old Babylonian records from that era indicate that a male worker's take-home pay for a day's labor was rarely more than one or two pounds [of grain]." Here Ruth (a foreigner *and* a woman!) is bringing home "the rough equivalent of a half-month's wages or more"—from just one day of labor![10]

4. What four things do we learn about Ruth's work in verses 17-18?

1. _____

2. _____

3. _____

4. _____

**Harvest and Ingathering,
Based on Modern Agricultural Practices in Israel**

	Mar	Apr	May	Jun	Jul	Aug	Sep	Oct	Nov
Wheat			●						
Barley		●							
Oats			●						
Peas		●	●						
Chickpeas				●					
Lentils		●	●						
Vetch		●	●						
Sesame					●				
Flax					●				
Millet					●	●			
Grapes				●	●	●	●		
Figs						●	●		
Pomegranates						●	●		
Olives							●	●	●

If the sun set in ancient Israel around the same time it does in Israel today, sunset during the harvesting month (April) would have been a little after 7:00 p.m. The word 'ereḇ (עֶרֶב, pronounced *eh-reb*) in verse 17 means just what is translated into English: "evening, night, sunset."[11] This means that Ruth worked from morning (verse 7) until evening, first finishing picking up stray sheaves of barley, then, after it was dark, starting the tedious and laborious task of threshing and winnowing (getting the actual barley seeds from the dried, yellowish grassy stalks). Ruth likely worked long past the last harvester headed home.

I imagine her sitting once the winnowing and threshing was complete, tears streaming down her dirty cheeks. Exhausted and overwhelmed by Boaz's graciousness and God's radical love for two poor widows, she heaves the heavy satchel upon her back and limps home on tired feet.

As the door swings open and Ruth stumbles in after walking miles from the farm all the way into town with her massive bag full to the brim, Naomi must have stared with wide eyes. Tears probably welled up in her own eyes as she took in the sight: the sack full of barley and the leftovers from the meal Boaz's team shared with Ruth (I wonder if he gave her a double portion, knowing she'd save some for her mother-in-law).

Ruth's radical love, the intense sacrifices of back-breaking work and exhaustion, spilled over into radical love from Boaz as he offered some of what he had to care for these women. What could have compelled Ruth to make such a sacrifice, on top of the sacrifice of moving from her home to care for her widowed mother-in-law? For she was not only caring for herself, gleaning just enough to get by—she was going to extravagant lengths to provide for the family she had left.

And this love, this selflessness, does something we could not have imagined to the broken woman standing before Ruth.

5. Look back at Ruth 2:20, and compare it to Naomi's words in Ruth 1:20-22. What do you think is going on? Why the change?

You either get better or you get bitter. It's simple. You either take what has been dealt to you and allow it to make you a better person, or you allow it to tear you down.
JOSH SHIPP

Hardship can make us better or it can make us bitter. Naomi chose the latter. Why do I say *chose*? Did we just observe in day 1 that Naomi out-Jobed Job?

Well, consider what we don't see—what's happening in the spaces between the lines of the story so far. As Ruth and Naomi walked the fifty miles from Moab to Bethlehem, they crossed the River Jordan, walked the sun-drenched desert, and then traversed steep mountainous terrain. Without a male chaperone, this would have been an especially dangerous trip, taking these weary travelers seven to ten days on foot. Did Naomi not see God's goodness in that safety? Did she not notice the love that walked in step with her along the way? Did she not care how excited the community was when they realized she was home? Ruth 2:18 says Naomi was in town, meaning they had found somewhere to stay. Yes, she had faced unimaginable tragedy. But God had not abandoned her. She chose to focus only on what she had lost, not on the ways He continued to care for her.

When Ruth comes home with so much grain and Naomi suddenly turns from anguish to celebration, it seems odd. How could someone who has worn a cloak of depression for so long suddenly be ready to throw confetti around the room?

6. How might Ruth's consistent love and sacrifice have been working in Naomi's life? Have you ever seen a shift in someone's outlook (even your own) because of someone else's faithfulness?

Maybe it had finally clicked. Maybe all those days of Ruth's faithfulness and radical love had finally settled into Naomi's soul. Maybe it was less about the amount of barley Ruth came home with and more about the overwhelming evidence that God's hand had not left Naomi after all. Ruth carried love over and over into Naomi's darkness—her own love, Boaz's love, and the Almighty's boundless and fathomless love. God shows up in the love we bring to the world.

> Naomi said to her daughter-in-law, "Why, GOD bless that man! GOD hasn't quite walked out on us after all! He still loves us, in bad times as well as good!"
>
> RUTH 2:20, MSG

Talk to the Lord about where you can carry love into someone else's darkness. Pour your heart out to Him as you ponder how He wants to show up through the love you bring to the world.

_____

_____

_____

_____

_____

_____

_____

_____

_____

_____

_____

_____

_____

_____

_____

Amen.

WEEK 3 • *Day 3*

LISTEN
Place your phone over the QR code for this week's sacred song.

READ RUTH 3–4

You know how some stories stay with you? A few years ago, after a day of meetings with my publishing team, I returned to the parking lot to discover that my car wouldn't start. After an unsuccessful attempt to jump my Jeep (resulting only in my publisher and me nearly being electrocuted and laughing like crazy), I finally called a tow truck. But you know what? There are many horrible places to be stuck waiting for a tow. A place where you can snag free books is not one of them. I grabbed one and settled in for the long wait for the driver. That book ended up being a story I couldn't shake.

Emily Foreman and her husband Stephen moved their family to a Muslim nation to share the extravagant and radical love of God. Christianity was illegal—yet under the cloak of working with an NGO in relief and development, the Foremans developed meaningful relationships and invested deeply in the community, helping the people around them to start a small business and climb out of poverty. And along the way, the Foremans got to love their new neighbors and share where their love came from—their deep connection to Jesus Christ.

But then, horrifically, one day Stephen was murdered for this work. Emily writes,

We faced a lot of storms during our time in this country, both natural and metaphorical. You know that phrase "God will never give you more than you can handle"? It's not true. But do you know what is true? God will never give you more than *he* can handle. We saw that in each and every storm. But some kinds of storms were harder than others.[12]

Emily later wrote, "Like James Calvert, missionary to the cannibals of Fiji, Stephen had lived by these words: 'We died before we came here.'" It was their family's mantra and constant refrain because they lived a life of radical love.[13]

1. Flip over to Romans 8:1-3 in your Bible or go online and read it in several translations until you feel like you understand it. What does this Scripture passage say about being set free?

_____

_____

_____

_____

Jesus set us free from death because He conquered it on the cross. In other words, because of His radical love for us, we have the opportunity to live with Him in life-giving relationship for eternity.

Digging deeply into Ruth's entire story in three short days just isn't going to happen—there's simply too much meat in here to unpack. That's why we're choosing to focus on one key aspect of who Ruth was and how she lived, because that one thing has profound implications for how we participate in the story of God.

For the past several days I've referenced Ruth's radical love. In ancient Hebrew, this concept is *hesed*. The word *hesed* (pronounced *heh-sed*) is used once at the beginning of Ruth, again in the middle, and one more time toward the end, a constant thread throughout the story. And although it's only mentioned these three times, the entire narrative is saturated with this beautiful word.

2. Flip to each verse listed below in your Bible and pen down how your version translates the word *hesed*.

Ruth 1:8

Ruth 2:20

Ruth 3:10

Your version likely uses words like *kindness*, *lovingkindness*, *mercy*, *goodness*, and *favor*. Sadly, our English language simply isn't robust enough to explain this Hebrew word accurately. One of our kids came home from school the other day with a worksheet full of words they're not allowed to use in English class. Words like *happy*, *nice*, *fine*, and *okay* were listed, with space for students to come up with more vibrant and colorful synonyms. I remember having a similar conversation with my teacher in high school. "*Nice* is a nothing word," she said. "It's an empty, lazy, filler word." This is kind of how I feel about the English words that are used to decipher what *hesed* really means.

Biblical literature professor Robert L. Hubbard Jr. wrote this about the people in the book of Ruth:

> They are ordinary people—people like the reader—who portray an extraordinary alternative to the way life is commonly lived, the life of *hesed* ("compassionate loyalty"), with appealing sincerity and simplicity.[14]

Compassionate loyalty. I like that. *Hesed* is not a fairy-tale type of love but something that can be shown to everyone. It's a putting-others-first type of love, a selfless love that asks for nothing in return. It's loving your neighbor as you would love yourself. It's literally the gospel in action.

3. As you read chapters 3 and 4, in what ways do you see *hesed* displayed?

_____

_____

_____

Boaz didn't give Ruth the opportunity to bring home a few weeks' worth of grain as a way to flirt with her. He didn't marry her because Cupid had shot any arrows. Instead, he acts out of *hesed*, in direct contrast to a story we read earlier in this study.

4. Remember when we learned about levirate marriage in Tamar's story? What is a levirate marriage? (Feel free to flip back to Tamar's story in week 1.) How is Boaz's response to Ruth different from Onan's to Tamar?

_____

_____

_____

_____

 History Lesson

Let's talk about the difference (and confusion) between a levirate marriage (Deuteronomy 25:5-10) and a kinsman-redeemer (Ruth 2:20; *gā'al*, pronounced *gah-al*). They're similar, yet utterly different.

When Israelites settled in the Promised Land, Joshua (well, technically God and Joshua) gifted land to tribes and families.[15] This land stayed with the family from generation to generation, which is one of the reasons genealogies and family lines were so important.[16]

Under this system, a property would not be sold outright—instead, it would have terms somewhat like a lease agreement. This agreement provided pathways for the land to one day be returned to the family. The law of the jubilee (see Leviticus 25:8-17) commanded that land be returned to the original owners every fifty years, but a more direct means was that of the kinsman-redeemer.[17] The kinsman-redeemer could redeem the property back to the original family. This was a massive responsibility—it wasn't just about getting the land but also involved taking care of the larger family, including the people (such as a widow) connected to the land.

> If your brother becomes poor and sells part of his property, then his nearest redeemer shall come and redeem what his brother has sold. If a man has no one to redeem it and then himself becomes prosperous and finds sufficient means to redeem it, let him calculate the years since he sold it and pay back the balance to the man to whom he sold it, and then return to his property.
>
> LEVITICUS 25:25-27

Unlike Onan, who used a levirate marriage to take advantage of Tamar, Boaz offers a levirate marriage as a beautiful act of *hesed*. The difference with a kinsman-redeemer is that the wife is just a bonus, a responsibility that comes with the family land.

Remember in Ruth 4:5-6 when the original redeemer wants the

land but not Ruth, so he turns the deal down? We might look down on this guy as selfish and small-minded, and perhaps he was—but the information we're given within the context of our story simply shows that he's pragmatic and sensible, recognizing the full implications of the decision. He knew this decision would affect the family he already had. Gaining a field simply wasn't worth also gaining a wife (and the disruption her first-born child would bring his inheritance and family legacy). I don't blame him one bit.

The interesting thing with this portion of the story is that Boaz didn't have to do a thing. Yes, Ruth approached him on the threshing floor on that fateful night. Yes, she proposed marriage (gasp!), which was one step further in the conversation than even her mother-in-law had suggested. None of those things obligated him to be her kinsman-redeemer, though.

But Boaz shows himself to be a kind, generous, faithful, *hesed*-filled man. And it's not just that he agreed to marry the widow of a distant relative. That widow was an outsider, a Moabite. She would have faced prejudice after moving to Bethlehem. People would have looked at her, from a nation that was Israel's enemy, with suspicion.

5. Why do you think (other than pure, unadulterated *hesed*) would Boaz not worry about the fact that Ruth was a Moabitess?

Ruth has obviously proven that she is a woman worthy of praise. Toward the end of the story, the townswomen even declare her to be worth more than seven sons (Ruth 4:15). Boaz himself had already heard of her reputation, as we know.

6. But there's another reason. Let's look back at the genealogy of Jesus. Who was Boaz's mother?

Boaz's legacy is already diverse. He understands that a woman's past isn't necessarily her future. He knows that God can rescue and redeem people from any place and any people. He gives second chances because he's seen the Lord give second chances. He sees incredible value in Ruth because of who she is as a person, not because she has a certain pedigree or background.

But something truly extraordinary is happening here—something that takes the *hesed* of both Ruth and Boaz to the next level.

You see, levirate marriage would have extended itself to Naomi, not Ruth. Boaz was a relative to Elimelech and therefore the obligations of providing a son were for Naomi, not Ruth. In the same way, the kinsman-redeemer law would have extended to Naomi, not Ruth. The field was Naomi's husband's, and was to be redeemed on behalf of Naomi, not Ruth. And this has big implications for what happens next:

> Whoever redeems Naomi's land must siphon off resources from his own estate to purchase and then rehabilitate Elimelech's overgrown fields. If Ruth gives birth, the kinsman-redeemer who fathers her child faces financial ruin because everything he's invested, along with Elimilech's estate, will go to her child. As a result, he will leave to his own sons a fraction of what he would pass on by simply keeping things as they are.[18]

7. Flip over to Ruth 4:13-17. What do we learn about the relationship between Obed and Naomi?

Carolyn Custis James points out the powerful sacrifice that is happening here:

Even with the birth of Obed, Ruth continues sacrificing for Naomi. Anyone would say that after everything Ruth did for Naomi, it was time for her to enjoy a little happiness herself. Marriage to Boaz and the birth of a son seem fitting rewards for such an extraordinary and selfless woman. But Ruth still isn't thinking of herself. She has never veered from her vow. Here at the last, in the final and greatest sacrifice of all, Ruth gives up her child. The story ends, not with a disappointing thud but with a powerful gospel moment.[19]

Let that sink in for a minute. Ruth was, in effect, becoming a surrogate for Naomi. She would bear the child, but he would be Naomi's son.

8. Can we talk about Tamar again real quick? Because she's brought up here toward the end of chapter 4. Read Ruth 4:11-12. What do these words indicate about the people's perspective—now many generations removed—of our girl Tamar?

If Tamar were a conniving seductress . . . would they really use her name in a blessing over the union of Ruth and Boaz? No way! This just shows that ancient Israel truly did see Tamar as righteous. We may never be able to fully understand her actions, but they did. King David even named one of his daughters after this great-great- (many greats) grandmother.

God was the hero of Tamar's story, and He is the hero of Ruth's story as well. Boaz foreshadows the coming of Jesus, giving us a little preview of how He will treat the widow, the foreigner, the dejected (and how we should too). Boaz gives us a glimpse of the love Jesus has for women, especially those who have been cast aside.

In Christ's family there can be no division into Jew and non-Jew, slave and free, male and female. Among us you are all equal. That is, we are all in a common relationship with Jesus Christ. Also, since you are Christ's family, then you are Abraham's famous "descendant," heirs according to the covenant promises.

GALATIANS 3:28-29, MSG

But the source of this *hesed*, the person who draws it out of everyone around her through her own compassionate loyalty, is Ruth. Ruth acts in astounding, others-focused ways at every point in this story. And her love changes the trajectory of her family and places her right in the middle of God's story of redemption.

9. *Hesed* cannot be static or complacent. It is a word quivering with action. *Hesed* is something you do, a way you live. How are you living a life of *hesed*? Or how would you *like* to be?

Hesed extends beyond typical borders and creates a world full of love lavishers and grace givers. It's not about who's worthy and deserving—it's about how you want to love and live. The kind of legacy you want to leave. And becoming increasingly like the One who has shown you *hesed* as you follow Him into the story He's writing.

I will praise you, Lord. . . . For great is your love [*hesed*], reaching to the heavens.

PSALM 57:9-10, NIV

I will sing of your strength, in the morning I will sing of your love [*hesed*].

PSALM 59:16, NIV

You, Lord, are forgiving and good, abounding in love [*hesed*] to all who call to you.

PSALM 86:5, NIV

Give thanks to the LORD, for he is good; his love [*hesed*] endures forever.

PSALM 107:1, NIV

[Boaz said,] "GOD bless you, my dear daughter! What a splendid expression of love! And when you could have had your pick of any of the young men around. And now, my dear daughter, don't you worry about a thing; I'll do all you could want or ask. Everybody in town knows what a courageous woman you are—a real prize!"

RUTH 3:10-11, MSG

Talk to the Lord about how you can offer *hesed* to your family, friends, and community. Pour your heart out to Him as you ponder how He's inviting to participate in His restoration and redemption.

Amen.

Bathsheba

A Woman Who Claims Her Voice

WEEK 4 • *Day 1*

LISTEN
Place your phone over the QR code for this week's sacred song.

READ 2 SAMUEL 11:1-4

NOTE: Before diving in, I want to acknowledge that this week covers some difficult territory that may be painful for some. If discussion of sexual assault and abuse of power sparks memories and trauma, I want to hold space for you. To determine whether you wish to proceed with this week, I'd recommend having a trusted friend, family member, or even counselor simply read through these next three days (it shouldn't take them long, since they're not doing the study). Then, after they've shared their thoughts, prayerfully consider how you'd like to proceed. If you decide these chapters aren't for you, that's okay. Taking care of yourself is more important than finishing every last bit of a Bible study. I love you and want to make sure this remains a safe place for you.

In between my sophomore and junior years of college, I took a year off to attend Capernwray Bible School in the Lake District of beautiful England. On my flight home during Christmas break, I settled into the bulkhead seat toward the front of the plane, thrilled that the many hours I'd spend in the air from London to Washington, DC, would be spent with loads of legroom. Headphones and cozy socks on, and a big fluffy blanket scarf on my lap, I settled in, enjoying a book.

Until halfway through the flight, when I felt hot breath on my neck. I glanced over, and the man in the seat next to me was so close, the little hairs on my arms stood up in full red-flag alert. I'll spare you the details, but I quickly realized that this man had had more than his share of in-flight alcohol. Hour upon disgusting hour, I was stuck sitting next to this toxic and dangerous man as he propositioned me with vulgar words and actions.

Yes, I asked him to leave me alone. Of course I did. But I was afraid to make a scene. Nice Christian girls don't make scenes, right? (Wrong.) I was shy, insecure, unprepared for what to do in this sort of situation. I shot pleading glances at the flight attendant who, over the many hours I endured this abuse, often glanced our way with concern. I never asked to be moved. She never came to move me. I felt alone, scared, and voiceless.

I've shared this story with my girls, though they're not even in middle school yet. I want to prepare and embolden them in a way I wasn't. I want them to know that it's absolutely okay to make a scene. And I want them to know they have a voice and the power to speak up.

Women have faced assault and violence throughout human history. Today in the United States, someone is sexually assaulted every sixty-eight seconds, and most of those people are women.[1] Sexual assault is traumatic, terrifying, and destructive to the human soul. And fundamentally, this kind of assault isn't about sex—it's about power. It's one human silencing the voice of another.

Which is why, for those of us who have been victims of sexual violence, harassment, or abuse, reclaiming our voice is part of healing and restoration.

That brings us to David and Bathsheba. Even if you're new to this whole Jesus thing, you've probably heard the story: From the roof of his palace, King David sees Bathsheba bathing and tells his men to fetch her; he sleeps with her; she then becomes pregnant. In a vain attempt to cover his tracks, David comes up with a creative but unsuccessful scheme. Nothing goes according to plan, and in desperation he decides to arrange for Bathsheba's husband to be "accidentally" killed in battle so David can bring her in as his wife.

A lot of people talk about Bathsheba like she's a seductress, a Jezebel-type scheming woman. Or, at least, complicit in a sordid affair. "Why didn't she say no?" I've heard people ask. "Why did she *allow* this to happen?"

But . . . we already know women in this cultural context had little to no power. Do we really think Bathsheba had a choice when David's messenger came to her door?

In 2 Samuel 11:2-3, we read,

> ²It happened, late one afternoon, when David arose from his couch and was walking on the roof of the king's house, that he saw from the roof a woman bathing; and the woman was very beautiful. ³And David sent and inquired about the woman. And one said, "Is not this Bathsheba, the daughter of Eliam, the wife of Uriah the Hittite?"

David was at home while his army was at war. This was not unheard of for a nation's king—but it was unusual for David. He was a soldier, a fighter, a hero-warrior. But instead he stayed behind.

David had so many opportunities to change the trajectory of his choices. He could have gone to war. He could have chosen—as he walked on his palace roof, high above the rest of the city²—to look away when he saw a woman bathing below. He could have chosen not to let his lust drive his decision to ask about her. He could have chosen to respect Bathsheba's marriage when he found out she was Uriah's wife. He could have chosen to respect Bathsheba as an image bearer of God before he used her for his own sinful desires.

Bathsheba, on the other hand, was right where she was supposed to be, doing what she was supposed to do. She was in her home, following the law in cleansing herself at the end of her period. But a knock at the door, and Bathsheba's life would change forever.

Some shame Bathsheba for not saying no, for not turning away the messengers. But could she have?

1. Flip over to Esther 1 and read verses 1-12. What are the differences and similarities between Bathsheba's situation and Queen Vashti's situation?

_____

_____

_____

_____

Remember, in ancient cultures, women did not have a voice. As we saw last week with Ruth and Naomi, they had protection and security only when a man in their life granted it. Vashti was a queen, with more power than the average woman, and she tried to stand up for herself. (By the way, this wasn't just a woman being stubborn and not showing up at her husband's party—many theologians believe the king was demanding she parade naked before a party full of drunk men.[3])

Bathsheba had none of Vashti's power, none of the status to make her believe she had any option to say no. Her husband was away at battle. The most powerful man in the world demanded her presence. She was utterly alone.

2. Read Esther 1:13-20. What happened after Vashti refused the king's orders?

_____

_____

_____

_____

Let's unpack this. The queen said no—and she was stripped of her crown and set aside as a royal edict went out to the entire land, commanding that "every man is master of his own house; whatever he says, goes" (Esther 1:22, MSG). We're talking about the *queen* here.

3. What do you think would have happened to a lowly and humble wife of one of David's soldiers had she said no to the king?

_____

_____

_____

_____

The fear Bathsheba must have felt—the king demanded her presence, a man who could punish her for refusing. And not only that! We know from later in her story that he wasn't afraid to use his power to harm others in her life as well. Everything Bathsheba knew would have been at risk. This was coercion, pure and simple. It's not a matter of consent when the power differentials are this stark:

A man with all the power. A woman with none.

Read 2 Samuel 11:4 below and circle the four actions surrounding what happened to Bathsheba.

David sent messengers and took her, and she came to him, and he lay with her. (Now she had been purifying herself from her uncleanness.) Then she returned to her house.

- Messengers took her.
- She came to him.
- He lay with her.
- She returned to her house.

Biblical scholar Wilda C. Gafney tells us:

That she "came to him," conjoined with "he sent messengers to take her" in 2 Samuel 11:4, simply suggests that she walks along with the messengers rather than that she is stuffed in a sack or carried aloft to be brought to him. To come when beckoned by the king does not imply consent.

I argue that Bathsheba's going with David's soldiers on her own two feet should in no way be read as consent, but rather as holding on to a shred of dignity by not being dragged or carried out.[4]

God called David a man after His own heart. But here we see David far from the heart of God. He didn't just slip into sin—he sinned against Bathsheba in significant, destructive ways.

4. Have you ever been wounded or sinned against by someone who was supposed to be a Christlike leader? How was the impact of that wound different from ways you may have been hurt by others not in that position?

The apostle Paul wrote that teachers and leaders in the church will be "judged more strictly" (James 3:1, NIV). And while these words were written long after David was king, the truth beneath them is the same. Leaders who claim the name of God can not only wound in emotional, mental, or physical ways—they can have a destructive impact on the spiritual health of the people around them. When someone leads others—in David's case, a whole nation—under the name and authority of God, their sin can harm someone's understanding of who God is and potentially their trust in Him.

That's why I think we see Jesus show a different way in how He treated the vulnerable, those whom the world overlooked and mistreated. He showed us what the heart of God really is and what it means to be people after God's own heart.

5. How was Jesus' treatment of women different from David's treatment of women?

Throughout the Gospels we read many stories of Jesus' obvious value and affirmation of women. He regularly addressed them while in public (Matthew 9:22; Luke 7:12-13; John 4:27; 8:10-11; and so on)—generally a big no-no. He gave them a voice to share His Good News (John 4:28-29, 17:19-20). He allowed them to sit at His feet as His disciples (Luke 10:38-42).

What's more, Jesus honored women by giving them significant, paving-the-way, changing-the-game roles in His story, over and over.[5]

- *Luke 1:35*: A woman (Mary) was the first to receive news of the Messiah's human birth.
- *Luke 2:36-38*: A woman (Anna) first comprehended and announced the good news about Jesus.[6]
- *John 2:1-11*: Jesus performed His first miracle after a woman's (Mary's) request.
- *John 4:25-26*: A woman (the Samaritan woman) was the first person Jesus revealed himself to as Messiah.[7]
- *John 4:39-42*: A woman (the Samaritan woman) was Jesus' first non-Jewish convert.[8]
- *Luke 24:1-12*: A woman (Mary Magdalene) was the first person Jesus revealed Himself to after His resurrection.
- *Matthew 28:1, 10*: Jesus first appointed women (Mary Magdalene and "the other Mary") to "go and tell" of His resurrection.

During the time Jesus walked the earth, the voices of women were still being silenced, overlooked, not valued. And Jesus created space for women to speak. He saw them. He valued them. God's heart for women is not for us to be silenced, not for us to be powerless in the face of the powerful, but to take our place, to rise up, and to speak.

Generations before Jesus' birth, Bathsheba experienced the pain of how things were never meant to be. The sins of oppression, abuse of power, and taking advantage of the vulnerable profoundly harmed her life. But lacking agency and being forced into silence? These things aren't the end of her story. And it is not the end of yours.

6. Have you experienced feeling unseen, silenced, or not valued? How has that experience affected you?

The sinful Davids of the world do not define our story. The God of the universe proclaims over you:

Your voice matters.

God has given you a voice. And with that voice, you can set boundaries, lift others up, love well, fight injustices, and change the game. Let's use the voice we've been given, confident that the God who loves us wants us to speak.

Speaking out is often labeled as rocking the boat or causing trouble, but silence is just as dangerous.[9]
KATHY KHANG

If you feel unworthy or afraid to use your voice, talk with the Lord about that. Pour your heart out to Him as you ponder all your fears and experiences, all the moments your heart aches because you were not acknowledged and heard.

_____
_____
_____
_____
_____
_____
_____
_____
_____
_____
_____

Amen.

WEEK 4 • *Day 2*

 LISTEN
Place your phone over the QR code for this week's sacred song.

 READ 2 SAMUEL 11, 12:1-15

It was a dream come true: I was going to see Norah Jones in person. Years ago, a guy I was dating at the time surprised me with second-row tickets, and we settled into seats so close to the stage that we could see the spike tape marking where performers would stand. But then, halfway through the concert, there was a sudden loud blaring: As Norah began "Come Away with Me," a fire alarm backstage began to go off.

Norah stopped singing for a moment, continuing to play the keys as she listened to someone speaking through her earpiece. Then she turned to us. "Don't worry," she assured us. She'd let us know if we needed to make an exit.

And then something beautiful happened. She changed the key and tempo of the song, blending with the alarm and continuing the song like it was completely purposeful and planned. Norah turned chaos and disruption into something rich and deep and impactful.

As she exited the palace, Bathsheba likely didn't see any chance for redemption or hope in the midst of her personal chaos. The trauma and shame weighing on her on that walk home must have been overwhelming. She had been silenced by the king's power, and now she had to be silent in the aftermath of his violation. Who would believe her? We've talked about how even today, people debate whether Bathsheba was a willing participant in adultery—and can you imagine living through this? If she spoke up, the king could say and do whatever he wanted. He could blame her, lie, claim she was making things up. She had no options. She went home, carrying the pain of this horrible violation.

And we have to sit with that for a bit. Norah Jones might be able to turn a fire alarm into an instrument, but none of us can snap our fingers and turn trauma and pain into something beautiful. But even if we have walked through something horrible—a function of our broken world but never of the God who made it—our God can pick up the pieces. He can hold them for us. And slowly, over time, as we let Him heal us with His tender love, He works to redeem and restore.

Yesterday we talked about messengers being dispatched to take Bathsheba to David. There's a horribly ironic detail here that we should note before we go further.

1. Head to the BLB and look up 2 Samuel 11:4. Tap on *Interlinear* and then on the word *lāqaḥ* (לְקַח, pronounced

lah-kakh). In the space below, pen down some of the definitions given.

_____

_____

2. Now scroll down to look at some of the cross-references. Which usage is most surprising to you?

_____

_____

I was taken aback when I saw the word *marry*. As Wilda Gafney observes, "There is a terrible irony in that the verb *l-q-ch*, "take," normally indicates marriage when a woman is its object; here it signifies the violation of marriage."[10]

We don't hear a single word from Bathsheba during this story until some time (though only one verse) has passed. She sends King David a message with three short words (two in the Hebrew language): "I am pregnant" (2 Samuel 11:5).

This is the first time we hear Bathsheba's voice. Her words are simple and straightforward and profoundly courageous. She knew she couldn't hide a pregnancy. But disclosing the secret to a messenger meant she was putting both her and her baby's life on the line. If David denied responsibility, she could be accused of adultery—and the punishment was death by stoning. She must have been so terrified, especially since she heard nothing but crickets in return. David reacted, but we don't see that he responded to her—at all. If the term *ghosted* had been used back then, she'd have thought this is what had happened, for sure.

But in 2 Samuel 11:6-25 we get to see behind the scenes. David may not have responded to Bathsheba, but her news put him in a desperate, horrifying spiral. He conspires and schemes to smooth over and hide what had happened. If he can just get her husband, Uriah, to come home and be with Bathsheba, the man would think the child was his and be none the wiser, right?

3. Based on what we read here, what kind of man do you think Uriah is?

Bathsheba knew nothing of David's plan. But perhaps she did hear that Uriah was brought home to speak with the king. How her heart must have dropped. What would she say? How would she explain? Yet he never came to see her. She never knew how he honorably refused the king's offer to let him go home. Unlike David, who stayed home from the war, Uriah insisted on standing with his fellow soldiers. He went back to the battlefield.

For weeks, possibly even for months, she heard nothing from the king . . . until the news of Uriah's death in battle.

4. We learn in 2 Samuel 11:26 that Bathsheba mourned her husband's passing. We don't know exactly how long this mourning period lasted, but let's dig into some cultural context to get an idea. Head to 1 Samuel 31:8-13. How many days did the valiant men fast in mourning over King Saul and his three sons (including Jonathan), who all died on the same day?

If Bathsheba officially mourned only for seven days, then David moved with horrible efficiency. He didn't take her grief into account—only his need for a cover-up.

David's cover-up, though, wouldn't conceal much at this point. Too many other people were involved in his actions: the messengers who accompanied Bathsheba to the palace; others who delivered David her message; others who took part in the conversations surrounding Joab and Uriah; Joab himself, who participated in Uriah's murder. A secret like this was just too big to not have entered the rumor mill. The consensus among theologians is that even Uriah caught wind of the betrayal—that his honorable refusal to see Bathsheba was a way to shove the concept of honor in King David's face.[11]

5. Flip back to 2 Samuel 11:27 again. What did David do after Bathsheba's mourning period was over?

Most translations say Bathsheba was *brought to his house*, but the King James Version says he *fetched her*, which just makes my stomach turn. Once again, she wasn't allowed a voice. I recognize she wasn't given many options, and this was better than a public stoning—but she wasn't asked, she wasn't given space to choose or even share her thoughts. She likely felt helpless and defeated.

6. Look again at the very last sentence in 2 Samuel 11:27. What "thing" do you think the writer was referring to?

David messed up in harmful ways at every point in this story, and I have a feeling God was pretty upset about all of it. In this case, however, the sentence immediately follows David's actions toward Bathsheba, indicating that the "thing" God was displeased with had to do with David's treatment of her. In effect, the writer is saying: *But the thing that David had done [with Bathsheba] displeased the Lord.* As awful as the murder of Uriah (and the other innocent men with him) was, as disgusting as the cover-up was, what God focuses on here is David's specific and ongoing sin against Bathsheba.

7. In 2 Samuel 12:1-15, God's focus moves to the big picture of how David has sinned. Nathan chastises David, and in verse 9 he tells David two things in particularly that God calls evil. What are these two details and why are they important?

Neither God nor Nathan is upset with Bathsheba. Scripture does *not* say, "But the thing that David and Bathsheba had done displeased the Lord." Nothing in God's response condemns her. If Bathsheba's silence in Scripture has allowed many to speculate about her motives, Nathan's statements to David make reality plain: Nothing is hidden from God, and He knew that David was wholly and solely responsible. This is the king desiring something and using his power to get it. As Kat Armas writes in *Abuelita Faith*, "This narrative is surprisingly common; many poor women fall victim to 'indecency' due to the unequal power relations they often exist within, leaving them with very little room for negotiation."[12]

There was no grand wedding or joy-filled reception to launch the beginning of happily-ever-after. Instead, their marriage was built on a foundation of trauma, anguish, heartache, regret, and sorrow. And Bathsheba's devastation builds greater still as her sweet, precious, baby son becomes ill and dies. I can't even imagine her grief, anger, and confusion. As Lysa TerKeurst observes,

Losing someone you love can cut into your heart so viciously it forever redefines who you are and how you think.[13]

Several years ago, one of our kids was in a bike accident on his ride to school one morning. When the bicycle hit the ground, the handlebars turned upward and smashed into his torso. We had no idea his liver was lacerated and he was bleeding out internally, but we did know something was seriously wrong. As I barely held it together on the elevator at Children's Hospital, the two women and little girl standing across from me were teasing each other and laughing. And I was mad. How *dare* they be happy? How dare *anyone* be happy when my little buddy was lying in a hospital bed alone and scared?

Then the trio got off the floor of the cancer ward. I looked closer at the little girl and noticed the cap covering up her bald head. And I broke inside. *Give this pain to the grownups, God. It just doesn't seem fair.*

I can't comprehend the grief of losing a child, but I can wrap my mind around the fear of it. My heart aches for Bathsheba.

But here in the midst of her pain, we see the first glimpse of hope in her story. Through devastating loss, David finally repents and turns focus off himself and onto Bathsheba (2 Samuel 12:24). The word used here when David comforts Bathsheba is *nāḥam* (נחם, pronounced *nah-ham*). Our English language doesn't have this exact word, which means we don't catch the full depth of what's happening here. If we check it out in the BLB, we see that the definition of this word includes repentance and deep sorrow.[14]

David is *gutted*. And the comfort that he offers Bathsheba is his repentance for the grief he has brought upon them both.

Their marriage may have begun in sin and trauma, but this is the turning point. David is not just saying he's sorry so he can move on with his life. Repentance is a deep change in a person, a turning away from the wrong they have done. David is called "a man after [God's] own heart" (1 Samuel 13:14) not because he never sinned—we know he did—but because he didn't stay in his sin. He recognized the depths of his evildoing and chose to move toward God instead. Here we see the very beginning of healing and restoration in Bathsheba's life, as David fully owns his sin before God and against her. And the next time we see her, we see the impact of that restoration: Bathsheba fully claims her voice.

> I speak not for myself, . . . but so those without a voice can be heard. Those who have fought for their rights. Their right to live in peace. Their right to be treated with dignity. Their right to equality of opportunity. Their right to be educated.[15]
> MALALA YOUSAFZAI

 Talk to the Lord about being brave enough to name your pain and ask for justice. Know your Father sees you and what you have gone through. He is fighting on your behalf.

Amen.

WEEK 4 • *Day 3*

LISTEN
Place your phone over the QR code for this week's sacred song.

 READ 1 KINGS 1:1-35, 2:10-25

This morning while I was in the shower (where naturally, I do my best thinking and praying), a phrase flew into my mind. Over and over, it swirled around, repeating itself. It continued like a broken record as I dried off and cozied myself into a favorite sweater and thick slouchy socks. I ran down the hall to my office before it faded into the busyness of the day:

The voices around you become the voices within you.

We become like the people who surround us. We are shaped by the voices we hear, over and over. We choose who we become when we choose whom to listen to.

The voices of others, particularly those closest to us, have a powerful impact on the trajectory of our lives. That's why it's important to bring into your inner circle confidants who emphasize that you're exactly enough while still encouraging you to keep growing. To surround yourself with friends whose voices speak life and shout louder than those who aim to judge or injure. Those voices empower your tongue to declare and proclaim everything you are and everything you need.

For so much of our story, Bathsheba has been battered by the voices of the powerful. She was taken by messengers. She has lost her first husband at a king's word and a general's order. She was married to that same king at his demand. She has suffered more than most people could bear, and the way forward would not be easy. But just because she has been voiceless and powerless in so much of her story doesn't mean she was destined to stay that way. She had a decision to make—the same each of us has when we face pain. Will we stay silent and become a victim of our suffering, or will we speak up and choose to change our story?

Bathsheba chose to change her story. How do we know?

1. What clues do we have that Bathsheba changed her story? Look at 1 Kings 3:4-15.

In the Old Testament, we read stories about David's many children. David married women from various places, some of whom were Israelites, but others who weren't. If David was the constant in these children's lives, then the mothers were the variables—and the way the children chose to follow God or not is a direct reflection on the women who raised them. And of all of David's children, we are told of only one who loved the Lord: Solomon, son of Bathsheba.

> When he was born they named him Solomon. GOD had a special love for him and sent word by Nathan the prophet that GOD wanted him named Jedidiah (God's Beloved).
>
> 2 SAMUEL 12:24-25, MSG

The Lord loved Solomon, and we learn, especially in the early years of his reign, what a man of good character Solomon was. Carefully read again through 1 Kings 3:4-15—and really reflect on the kind of mother who raised such a man.

Yes, we are never told directly of Bathsheba's love of God. The only early insight we have into her faith is how she was obeying the law when David saw her. But let's pay attention to the fruit of her life: Her son Solomon became a man of wisdom, while David's other sons (through his other wives) completely flew off the rails. One raped a half sister; another killed in vengeance, attempted a coup that nearly dethroned David, and then raped David's concubines on the very roof David had peered at Bathsheba from. Devastation upon devastation.

But Solomon grew to adulthood following God. This suggests that Bathsheba clung to God in her trauma and defied her wounding rather than let it define her.

2. How has God helped you defy your wounding?

Much has happened, and years have passed between the moment Bathsheba first used her voice and the moment in the story we step into today. She is different now. Time, life experience, and strength of character grew Bathsheba into a woman with confidence enough to use the voice God gave her.

We pick back up in the life of Bathsheba in 1 Kings 1, and we see right away how she's learned to use her voice. If you haven't already, please read 1 Kings 1:1-4, paying special attention to the details of the young woman named Abishag. We'll come back to her later.

As we continue with the chapter, we learn that:

> At this time Adonijah, whose mother was Haggith, puffed himself up saying, "I'm the next king!" He made quite a splash, with chariots and riders and fifty men to run ahead of him. His father [David] had spoiled him rotten as a child, never once reprimanding him. Besides that, he was very good-looking and the next in line after Absalom.
>
> 1 KINGS 1:5-6, MSG

Years before, Absalom had tried to overthrow David. Now, in 1 Kings 1, Adonijah is attempting the same. This time, though, David is an elderly king nearing death. The time to pass the crown to a son is at hand . . . and Adonijah has decided the next king should be him. Many events lead up to a coronation feast Adonijah throws for himself (as one does when illegitimately commandeering kingship). First Kings 1:9-10 tells us that "he invited all his brothers, the king's sons, and all the royal officials of Judah, but he did not invite Nathan the prophet or Benaiah or the mighty men or Solomon his brother."

At the beginning of Bathsheba's story, she was kept in the dark as events swirled around her. No more. Over time, she has become the one in the know, while David remains in the dark.

It takes courage to grow up and become who you really are.

E. E. CUMMINGS

3. Read 1 Kings 1:11-14. What insights does this give you about who Bathsheba has become and the role she plays in the kingdom?

___

We never see David's original promise to make Solomon his successor. Wilda C. Gafney tells us, "There is a tradition in rabbinic scholarship, the classical exegesis of Rabbi David Kimkhi, that the way in which David comforts Bathsheba after the death of their first child is to make this promise."[16] Whether this is true or not, it's a good reminder that there are loads of conversations and information not included within the pages of Scripture. Can you imagine how long the Bible would be if every single conversation were recorded?

But regardless, the conversation between Nathan and Bathsheba doesn't indicate that this was a sudden made-up plan to deceive David. Bathsheba doesn't ask any clarifying questions to ensure their stories matched up. Nor does she ask Nathan, "Are you sure we should do this?" Or, "What happens if we get found out?" She doesn't say, "Remember how God knew when David attempted underhanded actions? God will know we are, as well!"

Biblical studies professor Sara M. Koenig notes, "Nathan is more honest with Bathsheba than he is with the king, which suggests some level of comfort with her."[17] We glimpse in this short interaction the signs of trust, maybe even a friendship that has brought Bathsheba and Nathan to this important moment. Solomon, the boy God loved deeply. This child—whom Bathsheba and quite possibly Nathan have invested many years guiding, teaching, and training up to also be a man after God's own heart—has grown up and now has the opportunity to become king. And Bathsheba and Nathan are ready to advocate on his behalf.

4. Read Bathsheba's conversation with David in 1 Kings 1:15-22. What do you observe about her actions and words? What insights do we get into her priorities and instincts?

_____

_____

_____

_____

Bathsheba's conversation was not remotely a word-for-word repetition of what Nathan had instructed her to say. She truly had found her voice. She added her own thoughts and observations to Nathan's instructions, using her instincts about how David might hear the request to guide her approach. Wilda C. Gafney notes, "She is not a puppet reciting a script. She is a partner, improvising as necessary."[18] She already knew exactly what was going on with the rebellion and intended take-over of the kingdom. With courage and intelligence, she voiced the details freely to her husband.

It's striking that of all the people Nathan could have approached, he sought out Bathsheba to have this conversation with the king. This suggests that she held a place of authority and influence with her husband.[19] We know from the story of Esther that, in the ancient world, approaching a king without permission often had serious consequences (Esther 4:11), yet Bathsheba entered David's chamber unannounced. This freedom, paired with her confidence in reminding the king of a realigned succession plan, could mean David considered Bathsheba his first wife, though she was actually his eighth marriage. From powerlessness to priority and influence—Bathsheba's role has changed massively over the years. This is another clue as to why Solomon wasn't invited to the supposed coronation of Adonijah.

Tag-teaming in conversing with the king, Bathsheba and Nathan open the king's eyes to the deception and betrayal once again swirling around his family, and David decides to crown Solomon that very day (1 Kings 1:28-40). The sounds of celebration over Solomon's (real) coronation were so loud that the partiers at Adonijah's counterfeit feast wondered what was going on. Once they realized Solomon now sat on the throne, "all the guests of Adonijah trembled and rose, and each went his own way" (1 Kings 1:49). (I picture this as a slightly hilarious parade of nervous guests finding excuses to leave the table one-by-one and never return.)

Adonijah was a bit freaked out, as you'd expect: He sent word to the new king, asking that his half brother please not kill him (1 Kings 1:50-51). Remember that part of Bathsheba's request to David included her expectation that Adonijah would kill her own son. A rival to the throne was a danger. But Solomon shows mercy.

Sometime later, we are told that King David passes away and "Solomon sat on the throne of David his father, and his kingdom was firmly established" (1 Kings 2:10-12). In 1 Kings 2:13, Bathsheba reenters the scene one final time as Adonijah comes to visit her.

Adonijah asking for Abishag (his father's former caretaker) as his wife was a telltale sign that rebellion was once again brewing. He wanted what his father had had, which translated into a message that he would still, at some point, attempt to overthrow Solomon and take the throne.

5. Why do you think Adonijah went to Bathsheba with his request to marry?

Adonijah obviously knows that Bathsheba's words hold weight with King Solomon, but he seems to think she's easily manipulated as well. But—spoiler alert—Bathsheba isn't dim-witted. She's deeply perceptive and astute. Don't believe me? Let's dig into the text a bit more.

6. How did Bathsheba greet Adonijah? How did she respond to his request?

Our girl was intelligent, articulate, and wise. She seems to see red flags all over the place from the moment Adonijah walks up to her. She doesn't even pretend any niceties—her opening line is basically, "Ummmm . . . what do you want?" She listens to Adonijah, doesn't let on what she thinks of his request, and technically doesn't even promise to advocate on his behalf—she merely says she would "speak for [him] to the king" (1 Kings 2:18). Bathsheba was discerning: she knew Adonijah's history of deception and, though she likely hoped the direction of his heart had changed, she braced herself for the possibility that it had not.

7. As we read the last verses in the story of Bathsheba, we step into my favorite part. Reread 1 Kings 2:19-25. What two things did Solomon do when he saw his mother?

   1.

   2.

In a flip of expectation, the king bows to her. She doesn't bow to him. An interesting side note to include, right? The incredible honor bestowed on Bathsheba now is a striking contrast to how she was treated at the beginning of her story. As a mom of four boys and one rock-star husband, I have never had anyone bow before me as I've entered the room, but I *have* had them provide a seat for me. The symbolism of *this* seat, however, is different. Solomon is giving her a seat at a table women weren't invited to. As authors Liz Fosslien and Mollie West Duffy so eloquently put it:

> Diversity is having a seat at the table, inclusion is having a voice, and belonging is having that voice be heard.[20]

Bathsheba has a seat at the king's right hand. Her voice is valued and heard. Through his actions, her son has publicly acknowledged her as the most powerful woman in all of Israel. And Solomon is no mama's boy. The king who will later become famous for his wisdom recognizes wisdom in turn.

8. Who can you give a seat to? How can you affirm and support them publicly, elevating them and giving them a seat they may not otherwise have?

_____

_____

_____

_____

Okay, but hold on, you may be thinking. *Bathsheba gives Solomon Adonijah's request, just like she said she would. How is that wisdom?* To figure out what's going on, let's look at something that's a little weird in Bathsheba's interaction with Solomon.

9. What does Solomon say in 1 Kings 2:20? And what does he do right afterward?

_____

_____

_____

Solomon says, "Make your request, my mother, for I will not refuse you," *and then he literally refuses her!* What is *that* about? Weird, right?

Well, not really. Here's the deal: Like in her conversation with Nathan, Bathsheba doesn't act as a puppet, merely reciting what she has been told to say. Bathsheba approaches King Solomon in her own way, using her own words. She says she has a "small request"—and then she makes a massive, kingdom-shifting one. This is a spot where I wonder if we're missing the tone in the biblical narrative. There seems to be deep sarcasm in what Bathsheba is asking. Her "small request" basically mocks the idea. "Hey, son. How about we allow this union to happen so your brother can symbolize his intent of usurping the throne, mkay? Cool."

Solomon has such respect for his mother and what she has to say that he doesn't even ask any clarifying questions. He knows exactly what she is implying. And Bathsheba knows what he will do with this information. Solomon trusts her and the wisdom she holds, and he immediately commands that Adonijah be executed. In doing this, Solomon has secured his reign and Bathsheba fades into the background. But just because Scripture doesn't talk about her after this conversation doesn't mean she's become unimportant. Solomon wouldn't have brought in a throne for a single conversation. No, our girl Bathsheba has become the first Queen Mother, and with that rose an honor and tradition that remained until Babylon came through and the kingdom fell.[21] This celebration of the king's mother emerged from a woman who learned that she can do hard things, live through hard things, and become a woman with a voice because of those hard things.

> The most beautiful people we have known are those who have known defeat, known suffering, known struggle, known loss, and have found their way out of the depths. These persons have an appreciation, a sensitivity, and an

understanding of life that fills them with compassion, gentleness, and a deep loving concern. Beautiful people do not just happen.[22]

And, as a matter of fact, Bathsheba may make one more important appearance in Scripture—at the beginning of the famed Proverbs 31 passage.

Proverbs 31:1 (MSG) says, "The words of King Lemuel, the strong advice his mother gave him." But who is Lemuel? Oh, you know, probably just Bathsheba's nickname for Solomon.[23] The consensus among Jewish and Christian theologians is that the mother whose wisdom informed Proverbs 31 is Bathsheba. Do I need to give you a minute as your brain explodes? David named him Solomon (meaning *Man of Peace*), God—through Nathan—named him Jedidiah (meaning *Beloved of the Lord*), and (theologians believe) Bathsheba called him Lemuel (meaning *Belonging to God*).

Bathsheba's wisdom lives on. Her voice is still heard. Let's be women who claim our voice, who steward our wisdom and influence so it endures for generations to come. Our God has given each of us a voice. Let's be women who rise above our pain and speak—stepping into the story God is writing.

> *Whatever* challenges we encounter . . . we can handle them because of the Lord's strength dwelling within us. Our weaknesses really do not enter into the equation.[24]
> CYNTHIA HEALD

Talk to the Lord about where He's inviting you to use your voice and influence. He has created you to speak—don't be afraid.

Amen.

Mary

A Woman Who Says Yes

WEEK 5 • *Day 1*

LISTEN
Place your phone over the QR code for this week's sacred song.

READ LUKE 1:26-55

I'm living the life I thought I never wanted. I was going to live in Europe and work at a museum—and I definitely wasn't going to have children. I wanted to live as a wallflower, my introverted self comfortably in the background.

Well . . . that all went out the window! My life now is basically the opposite of my plan. I live in the loud, the chaotic, the bustling. I'm often outside my comfort zone, standing on stages and in other public spaces. I didn't get my doctorate and am not in the art world—and instead, I have six beautiful kids, four of whom were born in a land thousands of miles away. My safe little bubble burst long ago. Sometimes this unanticipated life is scary and painful, especially since at my core, I am still shy, introverted, and easily overwhelmed.

What changed?

I got usable.

I said yes.

> God is looking for people to use, and if you can get usable,
> He will wear you out. The most dangerous prayer you can
> pray is this: "Use me."
>
> RICK WARREN

This last extraordinary woman named in Jesus' lineage was also the one with the most direct connection to Him: His mother. Mary would say yes over and over. When I think about Mary—why in the world did God choose her out of any other woman in history?—I come back time and time again to this uncomplicated but massively impactful word.

Her entire life would be built on *yes*.

Sometimes we aren't quite sure what to do with Mary. We might think of her as a passive and quiet, lingering on the edges of Jesus' life. Art through the ages has often portrayed her as delicate and serene (and inaccurately white and blonde). We often imagine her as reserved and gentle, a presence next to the manger in nativity scenes and a footnote in the rest of Jesus' story.

But I'll let you in on a secret: We've got her all wrong.

The Mary of the Bible is not the Mary of your nativity set.

Mary was courageous, vocal, and strong. And she had a deep faith in the One she said yes to. That's why she said yes even though a pregnancy meant she could be stoned. Although she was betrothed (engaged) to Joseph, they were not yet married, and an unwed pregnancy was dangerous to a woman in this time.

Short of stoning, pregnancy outside of marriage carried incredible shame. Had Joseph allowed it, Mary would have gone through the ritual of *sotah* (also called the law of bitter waters).[1] According to Numbers 5:11-31, a woman suspected of adultery would be made to drink a mixture of holy water, dust, and the ink of the priest's written curse. If she was guilty, the woman would become sick and unable to have children. But if she did not become sick, she was exonerated. Talk about weird. (On a related note, we once had a babysitter who was terrified of our cat getting too close to our kids. She said it would steal their breath. What?!) As you might imagine, merely the *idea* of appearing before the priest for this ritual was incredibly shameful.

Upon learning she would become pregnant—as a virgin!—before her marriage to Joseph, Mary would have known what could happen to her. Mary wouldn't have known how Joseph would respond to her pregnancy. She knew she would be rejected by some in her community, gossiped about by many. Life would never be easy, her future unknown. But still she trusted that God would sustain her through the journey ahead. When I look at her response to God in contrast to how many heroes of the faith responded to God throughout Scripture—honestly, it's pretty extraordinary.

1. Flip over to Exodus 3:10-11 and Exodus 4:10-13. God was giving Moses a daunting, dangerous job, just as He did (through Gabriel) to Mary. What differences do you observe between Moses' reaction and Mary's response?

When God told Moses he was chosen to help bring freedom to the enslaved Israelites, Moses came up with excuses about why God should choose someone else instead. He focused on his own ability, forgetting that the only ability that matters when we're called to big things . . . is God's. Remember, God doesn't call the qualified; He qualifies the called.

But Mary, the woman chosen to carry the foretold Messiah and Savior of the world, didn't even hesitate. Her head must've swirled with thoughts and questions, but she only asks a single clarifying question: "How will this be, since I am a virgin?" (Luke 1:34). Mary's question was not an expression of doubt, but a posture of wonder. She was "in" without more information, trusting that God would tell her more when and if He needed her to know. When I really stop to think about that—wow, is that immediate trust extraordinary. I don't know about you, but if someone (even God!) is asking me to do something big, I'm going to need the when, why, and how right away.

God chose the right woman for the job. He knew she was both tough-skinned and tenderhearted enough to become the mother Jesus needed. That's why Gabriel greeted her with the words "Greetings, O favored one, the Lord is with you!" (Luke 1:28).

2. Grab your phone and head to Luke 1:28 in the BLB. Once in the *Interlinear* section, scroll down to the Greek word *charitoō* (χαριτόω, pronounced *kar-i-to-oh*). What does this word mean?

3. But let's dig deeper. What's the root of this word? When you've clicked on the word in the *Interlinear* section of BLB and entered the *Lexicon*, you'll see Root Word (Etymology): χάρις (G5485). Click on this root word *charis* (pronounced *kar-iss*). What do the definitions tell us about God's assessment of Mary?

Can you imagine hearing a messenger from God calling you this? Massively humbling.

4. What does Luke 1:29 tell us is Mary's initial emotional response after this greeting? Why do you think she reacted this way?

Gosh, I don't blame her. If an angel suddenly appeared to me and said I was highly favored and full of grace and that the Creator of the

Universe saw me as someone who abounded in joy, delight, sweetness, charm, and loveliness . . . I'd wonder what was up. Mary knew the angel was about to say something significant, and she couldn't imagine how it could include *her*. God and His messengers had said the words "The Lord is with you" to men like Moses and Isaiah and Gideon and Jeremiah, always as a precursor to a big, startlingly dangerous calling. Here she was, a young woman from a tiny town—who was she to receive such a message?

Luke 1:30 goes on to say, "And the angel said to her, 'Do not be afraid, Mary, for you have found favor with God.'" For years I figured Gabriel was telling her to not be afraid because she was a bit shaky and wide-eyed over an angel appearing before her—just as men and women through millennia (like Hagar, Daniel, and the Bethlehem shepherds) needed to hear those words when an angel appeared to them (Genesis 21:17; Daniel 10:12; Luke 2:8-12). But I wonder if Gabriel wasn't saying this because Mary had come unglued over his sudden appearance. Instead, perhaps he's speaking peace to her ahead of what he's about to tell her—the magnitude of the calling she's being ushered into. When I read, "Do not be afraid," I hear kindness in his voice. *Hey. Mary. Look at my eyes. Breathe. It's going to be okay. Don't fear. God is with you in this.*

Mary knew the story of Moses. She'd grown up learning about Tamar, Rahab, Ruth, Bathsheba, and countless others who trusted in YHWH, even through uncertain and overwhelming times. What God has done in the past, how He shows His character and faithfulness over the ages, gives us confidence in who He is and how He will work in the present. And so Mary doesn't flinch. "I am the servant of the Lord; let it be to me according to your word." Her faith and courage, her simple yes, changed history forever.

With this yes, Mary entered a season of suffering *for* the Messiah, long before the Messiah would suffer for her and all humankind. She couldn't see the finish line, or even the path just ahead. Yet she trusted God enough to know that He would light her way.

5. What has God asked you to say yes to that feels overwhelming or scary? How have you responded? What holds you back? What gives you confidence to move forward?

_____

_____

_____

_____

After Gabriel left Mary alone with her news, we learn that she eagerly hurried—*spoudē* (σπουδή, pronounced *spoo-day*, like *spa day* but with an *oo*)—to visit her elderly cousin Elizabeth (Luke 1:39-40). After receiving an awe-inspiring and unexpectedly holy welcome by Elizabeth and her unborn baby, Mary sings a song now known as the Magnificat. Mary—a humble young woman from the margins—is the first to proclaim the gospel story.

6. Head over to Luke 1:46-55. Then take a look at 1 Samuel 2:1-10. What is similar? What is different?

MARY'S MAGNIFICAT (LUKE 1:46-55) AND HANNAH'S PRAYER (1 SAMUEL 2:1-10)

SIMILAR	DIFFERENT

For generations, women had prayed and recited the words of Hannah, mother of the prophet Samuel (who guided King Saul and anointed David to someday be king). Hers was a song of thanksgiving and a reminder of God's power and plan. But Mary's version does something different. She sings of justice, of God's deep care for those who are oppressed.

In the book *The Real Mary*, author Scot McKnight says:

> By reading the Magnificat in context, we can imagine Mary to be wiry and spirited and resolved and bold and gutsy. Maybe we should call her Blessed *Valorous* Mary instead of the Blessed Virgin Mary. Some think of her as tender; we might instead think of her as tenacious. Some think of her song as a splendid piece of spirituality that could be tucked away in a pew hymnal, but her song belongs instead on the shelf with socio-spiritual songs of protest against unjust rulers.[2]

A socio-spiritual song of protest? A battle cry of liberation? Really? Yep. Mary's words were ones of revival. A rally cry for those ready for the end of injustice.

> He has scattered the proud and haughty ones.
> He has brought down princes from their thrones
> and exalted the humble.
> He has filled the hungry with good things
> and sent the rich away with empty hands.

AUTHOR'S PARAPHRASE OF LUKE 1:51-53, INSPIRED BY NIV

In 1979, the Council of Latin American Bishops stated, "The poor [referred to in Mary's Magnificat] do not lack simply material goods. They also miss, on the level of human dignity, full participation in sociopolitical life. Those found in this category are principally our indigenous people, peasants, manual laborers, marginalized urban dwellers, and in particular, the women of these social groups. The women are doubly oppressed and marginalized."[3]

Mary was from Nazareth. In Mary's day, it was the very definition of a nowhere-and-nothing town, with a population of merely two to five hundred people.[4] Not near any major trade routes. No significance in Jewish tradition. Far from the holy city of Jerusalem. This small, secluded agricultural community was also within the region of Galilee, which other Jews often looked down upon because of how many foreigners lived there (Matthew 4:15-16). John 1:46 tells us that upon first hearing of Jesus, Nathanael (who would later become one of Jesus' twelve disciples) asked, "Can anything good come out of Nazareth?"

Mary knew what it was to be unseen and forgotten. She understood injustices and felt the pain of Roman rule. Who could imagine that a poor, ordinary teenager from nowhere would be used to carry God's revolution into the world? As Kat Armas wrote in *Abuelita Faith*, "I've found that God often works this way: shaming power by using those least expected, those whom the world might deem weak or insignificant."[5]

Through the ages, Mary's Magnificat has become the song of all who are oppressed. Hers is a story of taking up space in a world that had none for her. The real Mary isn't fragile. She is a woman of tenacious strength.

7. Head over to Luke 4:14, 18-19. What similarities do you see between these verses and Mary's Magnificat? What is the power behind this liberation of the oppressed?

This same Holy Spirit who empowered Christ in His ministry came to Mary (Luke 1:35), and we see in her words in Luke 1:46-55 the same power and authority and mission that Jesus proclaimed. This was no tame, passive woman. God had chosen a warrior.

8. Read Luke 1:46-55 one more time. Do you see anything interesting about the verb tense Mary uses? What do you think it means?

This is not something YHWH *will* do. Mary has such confidence in God's message to her that she sings her Magnificat in past tense, declaring it done already. She is firm in her yes because she trusts the One who secured it. God, the voice for the voiceless, the advocate for the unseen, is worthy of our yes.

> How many came in contact with her, talked, and ate and
> drank with her, who perhaps despised her and counted her
> but a common, poor, and simple village maiden, and who,
> had they known, would have fled in terror?[6]
> MARTIN LUTHER

Talk to the Lord about what you are nervous to say yes to. Offer your fears and anxieties around what He may be inviting you into. Pour your heart out to Him as you ponder the warrior woman Mary really was. Pray that you, too, can become a woman with incredible trust in Him.

Amen.

WEEK 5 • *Day 2*

LISTEN
Place your phone over the QR code for this week's sacred song.

READ JOHN 2:1-11

I've always wanted to be a wedding planner . . . except for the "giving up my weekends" part. So when I got to plan my own wedding nearly two decades ago, there was no way I was going to hire anyone. This was my chance to be as creative as I wanted, and I loved every minute of it. We turned our evening into a winter wonderland, complete with huge hurricane vases filled with birch branches and sea salt that sparkled like snow. The time was filled with laughter, fun, and romance. I didn't want the night to end.

If we'd lived in ancient Israel, though, Ben and I would have been back the next day to party it up some more. Depending on the wealth of a family, a wedding celebration could last up to a week. Now that's my kind of wedding!

The groom's family usually hosted the days-long celebration at their home, providing food and drink for guests.[7] This was obviously a large undertaking! All but the wealthiest of families asked friends and extended family to help with the cost.[8]

If we ran out of wine at a wedding today, we might pop open a few extra bottles of champagne or ask the caterer to send someone to the nearest store. But in first-century Israel, running out of wine wouldn't have been a mere inconvenience—the host family would have faced "grave humiliation." Theologian Edward Sri explains: "To run out of wine at a wedding feast . . . signal[ed] that they were unable to fulfill their role as hosts adequately and that they lacked the social connections to preserve their honor."⁹ The family would be shamed and disgraced. So when Mary realized what was happening at the wedding in Cana, she understood the gravity of the situation— and the need to remedy it quickly.

1. Why do you think Mary went to Jesus with this problem? And why do you think Jesus responded the way He did?

Whenever something odd is happening in Scripture, we need to pay attention. Jesus first seems to resist His mother's request—"Woman, what does this have to do with me? My hour has not yet come" (John 2:4)—but then He performs the miracle anyway. Stranger still, Mary seems to ignore Jesus' initial response; she tells the servants to "do whatever he tells you" (verse 5).

There seems to be an unspoken understanding here. It kind of reminds me of the mother-son interaction we discussed last week, between Solomon and Bathsheba. Like in that conversation, much more is happening here than we can intuit from their verbal communication alone.

Also, can we talk about this "woman" stuff for a second? In our context, that's a rude way of addressing someone—shades of a guy sitting on his recliner in front of the TV, yelling, "Woman! Get me another beer!" But in ancient Greek, *woman* (*gynē* [γυνή], pronounced *goo-nay*) was a common way to address a female. It didn't indicate criticism or lack of affection. Jesus used the title "Woman" when tenderly drawing the Samaritan woman to faith (John 4:21), when forgiving the sins of the woman who committed adultery (John 8:10), and when appearing to Mary Magdalene after His resurrection (John 20:15).

But when we look at the larger story of Scripture, there might be something important happening when Jesus uses this word to address Mary.

2. There are only six times where someone addresses Mary directly in the Bible. Read Luke 1:30; Luke 1:42; Luke 2:34-35; Luke 2:48-49; John 2:3-5; and John 19:26-27. What do you notice about the ways people speak to Mary? How is Jesus different?

Jesus is the only One in all of Scripture to refer to His mother as *woman* (here in Cana and three years later as He spoke to Mary from the cross [John 19:26]). I wonder if there's a reason. Let's take a look at a spot in Scripture where this title *woman* is prominent.

Most of us haven't done an in-depth study of Revelation, and we might find a lot of it intimidating, confusing, and more than a little bit frightening. But Revelation connects us back to Jesus' interaction with Mary in John 2.[10]

Let's read Revelation 12:1-9, 13. If you use an app on your phone with multiple Bible translations, I encourage you to first read this passage in a reading version (something like *The Message*, *The Voice*, or *The Passion*). You're welcome to go back and read it again in the translation you typically study from, but at this point we're just trying to understand the concept and tone of what's going on.

3. Write down in your own words what is happening in Revelation 12:13:

_____

_____

_____

Okay, Teresa, you might be thinking. *What in the world does this have to do with wine at a wedding?* Stay with me. I promise there's a point.

4. Who do you think . . .
   the dragon is?

_____

   the child is?

_____

   the woman is? (Note: This can have more than one answer.)

_____

It's okay if you have no idea how to answer any of those questions. I've basically just thrown you into this prophecy without a ton of backstory. There's much more to these apocalyptic symbols, but in a nutshell: The dragon is the devil, the child is the Messiah, and the woman is Mary (who represents a larger group: the people of God as a whole.) As Brant Pitre writes in *Jesus and the Jewish Roots of Mary,*

> In sum, according to the Gospel of John and the book
> of Revelation, Mary is not just the mother of Jesus. She
> is also a second Eve and the woman of Genesis 3:15, the
> mother of the Messiah whose offspring would conquer
> Satan and undo the Fall of Adam and Eve precisely by
> dying on the cross.[11]

Okay . . . so what?

Jesus calls His mother *woman* to highlight that the timeline of the confrontation between the devil and the Messiah begins the moment His ministry does. Edward Sri points out the deep meaning of this in his book *Walking with Mary*:

> For Mary, the wine she requests is simply a festive beverage that will help the families involved keep custom for the wedding celebration. But Jesus sees that in order to provide this wine, he will need to perform a miracle that will reveal his glory and launch the public ministry of his messianic mission. And this will begin his march toward the hour of his passion.[12]

In other words, once Jesus begins His ministry, the clock begins ticking toward Jesus' death and resurrection, the hour in which the devil will be conquered (John 12:31-33).

Okay, hope you've got some coffee, because we've got more to dig into—and it might make your brain explode.

5. By the time He gets to the wedding, Jesus has already had a big week. Look at John 1:19; John 1:29; John 1:35; John 1:43; and John 2:1. How many days do you notice between his baptism and the wedding at Cana? What has happened on each of the days mentioned?

    1.

    2.

    3.

    4.

    5.

6. Flip to Genesis 1:1. What does it say?

7. What does John 1:1 say?

In the beginning was the Word . . . and the Word was God. John's words here aren't an accident. He's mirroring the language of creation, pointing to the reality that God was beginning a new creation, moving from the Old Covenant to the New Covenant. Things are changing, but everything seems so ordinary that we don't even recognize the upheaval that has already begun.

Brant Pitre points out the significance of this: "In light of such parallels, both Protestant and Catholic commentators conclude that the Gospel of John is modeling the first seven days of Jesus' ministry on the first week of creation in Genesis."[13]

THE SEVEN DAYS OF THE NEW CREATION

Day 1	Testimony of John the Baptist (John 1:19)
Day 2	"The next day" (John 1:29)—the Baptism of Jesus
Day 3	"The next day" (John 1:35)—Jesus meets Andrew and Peter
Day 4	"The next day" (John 1:43)—Jesus meets Philip and Nathanael
Day 7	"The third day" [after Day 4] (John 2:1)—wedding at Cana[14]

Crazy, right? It's incredible what we discover when we look at the whole of Scripture, and how the inspired writers connected each piece back to the bigger story God has been writing.

Jesus tells his mother the time has not yet come because she's asking Him to do something within a time frame that she likely didn't understand. Or did she? Call it mother's intuition, call it the Holy

Spirit, call it whatever you like. But what if, in the same way that Bathsheba and Solomon's conversation was spoken between hearts more than words, so was Mary and Jesus'? Jesus associates Mary's request for wine with this hour of his passion and death, and He responds this way because His public ministry hadn't begun. But when Mary comes to Him with the statement, "They have no wine" (John 2:3), she likely did it with a lump in her throat. By bringing him this observation she was telling Him she understood the time had come and she was ready to step into her role, as well.

Her role? But what would her role be? Well, in ancient Israel, queenship in the Davidic kingdom was bestowed upon the king's mother rather than the king's wife because kings usually had more than one of the latter (see 1 Kings 2:19-20; 15:13; 2 Kings 24:15; and Jeremiah 13:18, 20). Makes sense, right?

Think back to Bathsheba's story. When Adonijah approached Bathsheba in 1 Kings 2:13-17, he was asking her to act as an advocate for him before the king. This is what the queen of ancient Israel was known for: She served as a voice for the people. In other words, "members of the kingdom would bring petitions to the queen mother and she would present those requests to the king."[15] Understanding this historical reality sheds some biblical light on Mary's statement to Jesus here in Cana. Mary, too, acted as an intercessor (for the family of the groom) at this important celebration.

We're not talking about Mary being an intercessor in the way that some traditions do (praying to Mary). No—remember how in Revelation 12, the woman represented *both* Mary and the people of God as a whole? Think about the implications for what is happening here! Mary signifies a shift in how people relate to God moving forward. Each of us is commissioned as an intercessor now.

Now, at this point, you might be like, "An inter-what-er?" So let's unpack that. When I was in college, a guy came up to me one evening and said, "I'm interceding for you." (My first thought: *Is this how random guys hit on girls at a Christian university? Weird.*) But also, I had no idea what he was talking about! I ran back up to my dorm room and grabbed the dictionary off my bookshelf. My finger drifted down the page of *i*-words till I found the one I was looking for: *Intercession: a prayer on behalf of another person.*

I had prayed for other people for as long as I could remember, but somehow this word made it feel different. Bigger. As my faith continued to grow, I learned more what this word meant. When we intercede in prayer, we're not just petitioning on someone's behalf—this is also an act of worship. We're spending time with Jesus because He is the only one who can carry all the pain and hope and questions we have. Praying for others (intercession) is essentially communing with Him.

Remember what Paul wrote in 1 Timothy 2?

> First of all, then, I urge that supplications, prayers, intercessions, and thanksgivings be made for all people. . . . For there is one God, and there is one mediator between God and men, the man Christ Jesus, who gave himself as a ransom for all, which is the testimony given at the proper time.
>
> 1 TIMOTHY 2:1, 5-6

In other words, each and every one of us gets to go directly to Jesus and advocate for the needs of a hurting world. Only Jesus is the mediator between God and humans, but we are given the privilege of coming to Him with our requests. Mary is the first representative in a long line of others showing that God has changed how He connects with His people. No longer is it for a chosen few. We are all intercessors now.

You still with me? Okay—so back to our confusing interaction between Jesus and Mary. We've covered that this really *was* Jesus' time to begin public ministry (we can all agree it was—I mean, He's not going to disobey his heavenly Father by creating wine for his earthly mom) . . . so why in the world does Jesus say, "What does this have to do with me"?

8. Please tell me I'm not the only one confused. Why do you think Jesus may have asked this?

Remember how I said we need to pay attention whenever something odd is happening in Scripture? The reason is because it usually means we're missing something in our English translation! When something doesn't make sense to us, there's probably something else going on—in the history, context, or original language. In this case, "What does this have to do with me?" (*ti emoi kai soi*) literally means "What [is it] to *me* and to *you*?" or "What [is it] to *us*?" Someone might use this phrase in conflict or hostility (see Judges 11:12; 1 Kings 17:18; and 2 Chronicles 35:21), but it could also indicate confusion because two people see something from different angles (see 2 Kings 3:13; Hosea 14:8).

9. Which of these two uses do you think is happening in John 2? How does it clarify what Jesus is asking?

Jesus is asking, "Why is this important to you? It's different from why it is important to me. Do you see the distinction?"

Mary wouldn't be shamed for wanting Jesus to replenish a festive beverage for the host family. Jesus knew that this miracle would represent something far more significant. The wine Mary requests is messianic wine—the symbolic wine foretold by prophets in the coming of the Messiah:[16]

> On this mountain the LORD of hosts will make for all peoples
>   a feast of rich food, *a feast of well-aged wine,*
>   *of rich food full of marrow, of aged wine well refined.*
> And he will swallow up on this mountain
>   the covering that is cast over all peoples,
>   the veil that is spread over all nations.
>   He will swallow up death forever;
> and the LORD GOD will wipe away tears from all faces,
>   and the reproach of his people he will take away from all
>   the earth,
>   for the LORD has spoken.
> It will be said on that day,
>   "Behold, this is our God; we have waited for him, that
>   he might save us.
>   This is the LORD; we have waited for him;
>   let us be glad and rejoice in his salvation."
>
> ISAIAH 25:6-9, EMPHASIS MINE

> "Behold, the days are coming," declares the LORD,
>   "when the plowman shall overtake the reaper
>   and the treader of grapes him who sows the seed;
> *the mountains shall drip sweet wine,*
>   *and all the hills shall flow with it."*
>
> AMOS 9:13, EMPHASIS MINE

With an abundance of the best wine the guests will ever taste (six jars at twenty-plus gallons each [John 2:6]—that's 120 gallons, or around *six hundred bottles!*), so launches the abundance of Jesus' messianic mission and public ministry.

We don't know for sure if Mary understood the magnitude of

her request, but she knew enough as the first follower of Jesus of the importance to "do as He says." A woman who says yes doesn't keep it to herself: She shares and lives out her confidence in the One who can do all things.

> As with Mary, the key to our obedience might be a threading together of various yeses to our Father's invitations, one at a time, until they string into the treasure of a surrendered life.[17]
> ELISA MORGAN

Let's approach the throne on behalf of others, bringing before God the needs of those around us. Be the intercessor you're called to be. Pray to the King Himself.

Amen.

WEEK 5 • *Day 3*

LISTEN
Place your phone over the QR code for this week's sacred song.

READ MARK 3:31-35; LUKE 2:41-51; JOHN 19:25-27; ACTS 1:13-14

My family lived in Guatemala in the mid-1990s, during a time of huge civil unrest—we lived through two coups and were surrounded by guerilla warfare. We were vigilant about safety, and we were never supposed to be alone.

But that's how I found myself one Sunday after church. We spent much of our week at an English-speaking church filled with missionaries, embassy folks, and other families like us who had moved there for business. My favorite spot was the courtyard with the huge outdoor fireplace, where we middle and high schoolers would congregate after services. We'd laugh and chat for a while, but often my friends and I would run up the cracked, tiled stairs to sing where the acoustics were best. On this day, though, after singing my heart out, I walked downstairs to the courtyard and discovered that everyone was gone. A few staff members were emptying pews of discarded bulletins, but otherwise the church was empty.

This was a church where the deacons wore guns under their jackets and we had armed security guards with machine guns outside the old wooden doors, but none of them were here now. I knew I wasn't in the safest position—and since this was before cell phones, there was nothing I could do as I sat alone in that courtyard.

After several minutes, in sped my dad, apologizing profusely. He and my mom had gone home separately—my mom and brother rode with some friends and my dad drove home alone afterward. Each figured the other had me in tow.

As a parent now, I think about my own parents' panic when I read the story of Jesus in the Temple in Luke 2. Mary, Joseph, and twelve-year-old Jesus had traveled to Jerusalem for Passover. After celebrating and traveling home for a day, Jesus' parents realized their precious child was nowhere to be found. They, too, had accidentally left him behind. During those days, families traveled together for Passover and other festivals. Aunts, uncles, cousins, grandparents, extended family on both sides . . . they all traveled as one big, loud horde. It's not hard to imagine Mary and Joseph assuming Jesus was with relatives, only to discover too late that He was nowhere to be found.

> And when they did not find him, they returned to Jerusalem, searching for him. After three days they found him in the temple, sitting among the teachers, listening to them and asking them questions. And all who heard him were amazed at his understanding and his answers. And when his parents saw him, they were astonished. And his mother said to him, "Son, why have you treated us so? Behold, your father and I have been searching for you in great distress."
>
> LUKE 2:45-48

In case you're wondering why we're going backward in Mary's life from where we were yesterday, I promise there's a reason. This experience gives us a glimpse into what prepared her for where we're going next.

1. What in Luke 2:41-51 might have prepared Mary for where we find her in John 19:25-27?

_____

_____

_____

_____

2. How do both events connect back to Simeon's prophecy in
   Luke 2:34-35?

_____

_____

_____

When one of our sons was in elementary school, we lost him at a
5K for so long that police became involved in the search. We eventually discovered him wandering through the booths of the expo, filling
his swag bag with free snacks from the vendors, but that terror has
stayed with me. I can imagine what Mary may have felt scouring
Jerusalem for her twelve-year-old.

3. Mary says, in the second part of verse 48, "Your father and
   I have been searching for you in great distress." Let's head to
   this verse in the Blue Letter Bible and tap on *Interlinear*. How
   would you describe Mary's emotions during this story?

_____

_____

_____

The word used in Luke 2:48 is *odynaō* (ὀδυνάω, pronounced
od-oo-nah-o), which literally means, "to cause intense pain," "to tor-
ment," "to grieve," or "to sorrow."[18] This was no nervous searching.
This was full-on freak-out mode. And it would not be the last time
Mary would lose Jesus for three days. I wonder if both times she
thought back to Simeon's words when Jesus was only forty days old:
"A sword will pierce through your own soul also" (Luke 2:35).

Something important was happening here—something far more
significant than parents looking for a lost child. In ancient Israel,
honoring your father and mother was one of the top principles,
both culturally and spiritually. But even at twelve years old, Jesus

MARY: A WOMAN WHO SAYS YES   ●   153

was helping Mary understand the realities of who He was: that her relationship with Him was subordinate to His relationship with His heavenly Father. She was not simply His mother; she was His follower . . . and though it was a painful lesson, she needed to reposition her heart and continue to live openhandedly, trusting and relying on God, just as she had with her first yes.

But no one said it would be easy.

As Mary stood at the foot of the cross, memories likely swirled together with grief. She likely recalled the gravity and pain of losing her son twenty-one years prior, and she may have also remembered the time she and Jesus' brothers came to see Him in Capernaum.

4. Flip to Mark 3 and read verses 31-35. What is happening in this story? Why do you think Jesus responded this way?

I used to dislike this story because I didn't understand it. But this isn't like in high school when your best friend abandons you because they've found a cooler crowd. Jesus isn't turning His back on His precious mother—instead, He's again helping her to understand her place in the family of God and in relationship with Him. He was not reestablishing a Davidic dynasty in the way she thought He would. His Kingdom was no longer about bloodlines. Jesus was building a family based on adoption.

And really, adoption was part of Jesus' earthly story from the beginning. For Jesus to be the Messiah, He needed to be in the family of David and have a royal bloodline. But Mary didn't have that pedigree and heritage—Joseph did. Adoption brought Jesus into the family of David. And in Mark 3, He enlarged the family include to an even greater group. Jesus was creating a family that didn't necessarily look like Him or have the same background and upbringing as He did. Tax collectors, prostitutes, devout Jewish leaders, the poor, the rich, even those outside God's chosen people (Gentiles)—everyone was invited.

Once again, Mary had to be reminded of who her Son was. She needed to learn that what He was doing was far beyond her comprehension. She needed to continue to step forward and offer Him her yes.

As she watched her beloved Son hang on a cross, Mary would finally understand the deeper way of reading the Messianic prophecies. Yes, the Messiah would triumph—but first He would suffer *with* others, *instead of* others, and *on behalf of* others.[19] These two themes were somehow commingled, linking arm and arm, as if you couldn't have one without the other. As Scot McKnight has observed, "Suffering for others was a theme written into the very fabric of Jewish life, for the Passover observance itself revealed a lamb was to be slain to liberate the children of God."[20] This would be Mary's hardest yes—choosing to trust God even as she realized God-in-the-flesh was to become that lamb.

To the world, this does not look like success. This does not look like fulfillment of prophecy. Sometimes our yes feels like a step into the dark, a question of whether we will find God there waiting for us.

5. What does it look like to develop the perseverance to say yes over and over—even when your calling or life seems too much, too painful, or different than you thought it would look?

There at the foot of the cross, Mary was in the darkness. Every yes she'd offered her God had led to this moment.

And then Jesus spoke.

6. Read John 19:26-27. Write what is happening in your own words:

_____

_____

_____

Once again Jesus uses the title *Woman*. This time He does it with the intention of acknowledging the time has almost come.

The purpose of what He says is twofold, though. In one instant Jesus is announcing that they are coming to the end of the story, that the defeat of sin and death is at hand. In the next, Jesus also connects the *Woman* to the church as a whole: "behold, your son"; "behold, your mother."

7. Why is Christ's joining of Mary and John important? How does it connect back to what Jesus said in Capernaum?

_____

_____

_____

_____

This brings us to the final time we see Mary in Scripture. Shortly after Jesus ascends to heaven, we read these words:

> All these with one accord were devoting themselves to prayer, together with the women and Mary the mother of Jesus, and his brothers.
> ACTS 1:14

That's right—just before Pentecost, Mary is still saying yes. She is with the apostles, interceding in prayer.

But what's this about His brothers?

8. Check out Acts 1:14 in the BLB and look at *Interlinear*. What do you glean from the definitions and other ways the word *brothers* is used in Scripture?

_____

_____

_____

_____

This word can mean blood relative, belonging to the same tribe, or "brethren in Christ."[21] And while in this verse, the reference is likely to Jesus' blood brothers, we'll see that this same word *adelphos* (ἀδελφός, pronounced *ad-el-fos*) is used when Peter greets the crowd of 120 in the upper room (Acts 1:16). Through His death and resurrection, Jesus has linked together the family of God. Scot McKnight observes,

> The Magnificat's dream of a society governed by justice with peace streaming through its streets would come through the paradox of the Cross, the power of the Resurrection, and the life-giving creativity of the gift of the Spirit of God. The society of the Magnificat that Mary anticipated from the day Gabriel revealed it to her would come to pass in the Church. And in the middle of these church cells in Jerusalem was Mary.[22]

The young girl from Nazareth who said yes has grown to become the woman who still says yes. But now, she says yes even knowing what her yes can lead to. Even with knowing the pain of deep sorrow, even knowing that the road ahead would not be easy, she does not run away, does not say no, does not plunge into despair. Instead, she says yes to Jesus' commission from the cross, stepping into the broader family of faith, carrying the good news first entrusted to her by an angel out into the world:

Imagine the wilderness whooping for joy,
  the desert's unbridled happiness with its spring flowers.
It will happen! The deserts will come *alive with new growth
    budding and blooming,*
  singing and celebrating with sheer delight.
The glory of Lebanon's cedars and the majesty of Carmel and
    Sharon
  will spill over to the deserts.
The glory of the Eternal One will be on full display there,
  and they will revel in the majestic splendor of our God.

So, with confidence and hope in this message,
  strengthen those with feeble hands, shore up the weak-kneed
    and weary.
Tell those who worry, the anxious and fearful,
  "Take strength; have courage! There's nothing to fear.
Look, here—your God! Right here is your God!
  The balance is shifting; God will right all wrongs.
None other than God will give you success.
  He is coming to make you safe."

ISAIAH 35:1-4, VOICE, EMPHASIS MINE

And now, let us be women with the courage and hope to find our
place in God's story—
  may we be unafraid to pursue what is right and advocate for justice;
  may we dream big and stretch forward into the growth God calls
    us into;
  may we love fiercely and sacrificially;
  may we claim our voice and steward our influence wisely; and
  may we keep our eyes on the One worthy of all our trust, offering
    Him our brave yes
  again and again.
Amen.

When I stand before God at the end of my life, I would hope that I would not have a single bit of talent left, and could say, "I used everything you gave me."

ERMA BOMBECK

Which of these women's stories resonates most with your own journey? Where do you sense God calling you forward into His story? Pray it all out in the space below, knowing that He is faithful to draw you into the story He's writing.

Amen.

Acknowledgments

Through the years, as I've become an even more voracious reader (as if that were possible) and come to better understand the art of writing and being an author, I've started reading the acknowledgments . . . sometimes before I've even read the book itself. This is the peek behind the curtain, the understanding that it may take a village to raise a child, but it also takes one to birth a book.

So to my incredible husband, Ben, who has gifted me (many) days and weekends up at our little place in the mountains so I can get away and research, pray, and write without kids and chaos interrupting me 5,294,865 times a day: Thank you, my sweet love. I know being married to a writer is sometimes exhausting (because I hide out in order to dig in deep and get really great work done), but you do it with such selflessness. You are my favorite person in the entire world, and I'm seriously obsessed with you. You + Me = Awesomeness Forever.

And to our kids (Abreham, Ezekiel, Anton, Laith, Imani, and Elsabet): Thanks for knocking quietly and bringing me lunch or a snack when I've hunkered down so long that I've forgotten to eat. Thanks for not being embarrassed when I take you to the neighborhood pool and pull out five Bibles (different versions!) and thousand-page books on theology so I can study while you swim with your friends during summer break. Thanks for honoring the handwritten sign stuck to my office door with washi tape asking you to not disturb me when the door is closed. Thankfully, not every day is like this . . . but in my studying/writing seasons, you're kind enough to take it all in stride. Thanks for supporting me, loves.

To my other family—

Thank you, NavPress and Tyndale, for once again believing in this weird pink-haired girl who is obsessed with Scripture and teaching others about Jesus. Thank you to my dear friend and editor Caitlyn Carlson, whom I texted, emailed, and called too many times to count, not just about the book but about life. So thankful I get to be real-life friends with you as well as partner in yet another project. You know relationships are everything to me. Ginormous hugs and thanks to my other favorite people who believe in me so fully: my publisher, David Zimmerman; Olivia Eldredge; Elizabeth Schroll; David Geeslin; and Libby Dykstra. Thank you for making my books a thousand times better, for patience with me as I attempt to go in a million different directions, and for getting the beautiful final versions into the hands (and hearts) of those with whom the message will resonate.

Mom, Daddy, Erik, Caroline: Thank you for continued love, support, and encouragement as sometimes limiting beliefs creep in and I wonder, *Who do I even think I am to teach women when I barely even made it through high school?* (Hah!) Gosh, what doubt and insecurity can do!

Thank you to my best friend of well over two decades, Kiesha Yokers, and to Andrea Steinbrenner, Meredith Watkins, Kat Armstrong, Nirup Alphonse, and Anu Alphonse for also loving me well and talking me down from ledges. Writing can be a lonely job, but you all have supported me and allowed me to feel constantly in community and surrounded by my people.

Thank you to my sisters in the Open Door Sisterhood. To be enveloped in love and encouragement by women who walk a similar path has been paramount. Krista Gilbert, Alexandra Kuykendall, Vivian Mabuni, Lucretia Berry, Marilyn Vancil, Helen Hope Kimbrough, Krista Breilh, Kristen Kill, Monica Swanson, Sarah Bauer Anderson, Diane Thomas: Hugs, hugs, hugs. Always.

And most importantly, thank you to Jesus for Your grace and love as You call normal, everyday women like me—and the five women listed in Your genealogy—to be used in the great story You're writing. Thank You for not calling the qualified, but rather qualifying the called.

Being part of a community puts us in proximity to other strugglers—people who can reassure us that we are not alone, who can offer wisdom because they're familiar with the woods we're lost in, and who can benefit from the experiences and insights we've gained through the hardships we've endured.

Russ Ramsey, *Rembrandt Is in the Wind*

Notes

INTRODUCTION

1. Patrick Schreiner, "5 Reasons Matthew Begins with a Genealogy," Gospel Coalition, January 1, 2020, https://www.thegospelcoalition.org/article/matthew-begin-genealogy/.

WEEK 1—TAMAR: A WOMAN WHO PURSUES WHAT IS RIGHT

1. I talk more about this in my book *Beautifully Interrupted: When God Holds the Pen That Writes Your Story* (Franklin, TN: Worthy, 2018).
2. *The Tony Evans Bible Commentary* (Nashville: Holman, 2019), 100.
3. Vivian Mabuni, *Open Hands, Willing Heart: Discover the Joy of Saying Yes to God* (New York: Waterbrook, 2019), 13.
4. Cornel West with David Ritz, *Brother West: Living and Loving Out Loud* (New York: SmileyBooks, 2009), 232.
5. "What I Learned After Losing My Legs—Amy Purdy," *The Daily Goalcast*, April 3, 2021, https://www.facebook.com/watch/?v=2436512113160485.
6. "What I Learned After Losing My Legs—Amy Purdy."
7. See, for example, Matthew Henry's commentary on the subject: https://www.christianity.com/bible/commentary.php?com=mh&b=1&c=38.
8. Edward J. Bridge, "A Mother's Influence: Mothers Naming Children in the Hebrew Bible," *Vetus Testamentum* vol. 64, fasc. 3 (2014): 389–400.
9. Jean Zaru, "Biblical Teachings and the Hard Realities of Life," in *Hope Abundant: Third World and Indigenous Women's Theology*, ed. Kwok Pui-lan (Maryknoll, NY: Orbis Books, 2010), 123–137.
10. Scott Sauls, *From Weakness to Strength: 8 Vulnerabilities That Can Bring Out the Best in Your Leadership* (Colorado Springs: David C. Cook, 2017), 184.
11. *Encyclopaedia Britannica Online*, s.v. "Nancy Ward," updated January 1, 2022, https://www.britannica.com/biography/Nancy-Ward.
12. David Ray Smith, "Nancy Ward," *Tennessee Encyclopedia*, accessed February 3, 2022, https://tennesseeencyclopedia.net/entries/nancy-ward/.
13. Smith, "Nancy Ward."
14. *Encyclopaedia Britannica Online*, s.v. "Nancy Ward."
15. Olajumoke Adenowo, *Tamar: Destiny Attained Against All Odds*, Kingdom Dynamics for the Marketplace, Book 3 (Abuja, Nigeria: Infospektra, 2019), 27.
16. Carolyn Custis James, *Lost Women of the Bible: The Women We Thought We Knew* (Grand Rapids, MI: Zondervan, 2005), 111.
17. James, *Lost Women*, 111.
18. James, *Lost Women*, 111.
19. James, *Lost Women*, 111; and Adenowo, *Tamar*, 26.

20. For more on how we know the book of James was written by Jesus' half brother, see "Who Wrote the Book of James?," Zondervan Academic, September 6, 2017, https://zondervanacademic.com/blog/who-wrote-the-book-of-james.
21. *The Women's Torah Commentary*, edited by Elyse Goldstein (Woodstock, VT: Jewish Lights, 2000), 95.
22. James, *Lost Women*, 115.
23. Because Tamar's sons are listed in the genealogies from here on out, we know that Judah kept them in his household. In Genesis 43, we see that Judah has turned from his life in Canaan and rejoined his father's household. His sons would have come with him, along with their mother.
24. Adenowo, *Tamar*, 35.

WEEK 2—RAHAB: A WOMAN WHO CHOOSES GROWTH

1. Thesaurus.com, s.v. "shrew, *n.*," accessed February 4, 2022, https://www.thesaurus.com/browse/shrew.
2. *Collins Dictionary*, "shrewd, *adj.*," accessed February 4, 2022, https://www.collinsdictionary.com/us/dictionary/english-thesaurus/shrewd; and Lexico, "shrewd, *adj.*," accessed February 4, 2022, https://www.lexico.com/en/definition/shrewd.
3. Olajumoke Adenowo, *Rahab: Wisdom for a Quantum Change*, Kingdom Dynamics for the Marketplace, Book 1 (Abuja, Nigeria: Infospektra, 2019), 18–19.
4. Sarah Bessey, *Jesus Feminist* (New York: Howard Books, 2013), 155.
5. Ardie Myers, "From Rags to Riches: Author Reviews Life of Madam C. J. Walker," *Library of Congress Information Bulletin* 60, no. 5 (May 2001), https://www.loc.gov/loc/lcib/0105/glorifying_womanhood.html.
6. Debra Michals, "Madam C. J. Walker," National Women's History Museum, accessed February 7, 2022, https://www.womenshistory.org/education-resources/biographies/madam-cj-walker.
7. Tanya Dalton, *On Purpose: The Busy Woman's Guide to an Extraordinary Life of Meaning and Success* (Nashville: Nelson Books, 2021), 24.
8. Bessey, *Jesus Feminist*, 101.
9. Rachel Held Evans, *A Year of Biblical Womanhood: How a Liberated Woman Found Herself Sitting on Her Roof, Covering Her Head, and Calling Her Husband Master* (Nashville: Thomas Nelson, 2012), chap. January: Valor.
10. Gene A. Getz, *Joshua: Living as a Consistent Role Model* (Nashville: Broadman & Holman, 1995), 44–45.
11. For more on flax, see Liné Cowley, "Linen Fabric and Flax Cultivation," Eco World, June 3, 2019, https://ecoworldonline.com/linen-fabric-and-flax-cultivation/; Deborah J. Greenhill, "Biblical Accounts of Linen and Flax Seed," The——Thread, February 17, 2010, https://blog.fabrics-store.com/2010/02/17/biblical-accounts-of-linen-and-flax-seed/; and "Linen," BiblicalTraining, accessed March 16, 2022, https://www.biblicaltraining.org/library/linen.
12. Library of Congress, "Scrolls from the Dead Sea," accessed February 11, 2022, https://www.loc.gov/exhibits/scrolls/intr.html.
13. Greenhill, "Biblical Accounts of Linen and Flax Seed."
14. Blue Letter Bible, "Lexicon: Strong's H2450—ḥāḵām," accessed February 7, 2022, https://www.blueletterbible.org/lexicon/h2450/esv/wlc/0-1/.
15. "The heart is spoken of as being the seat of wisdom," Blue Letter Bible, "Lexicon: Strong's H2450—ḥāḵām," accessed February 7, 2022, https://www.blueletterbible.org/lexicon/h2450/esv/wlc/0-1/.
16. Getz, *Joshua*, 45.
17. William Evans, *The Great Doctrines of the Bible*, Section Two (Chicago: Bible Institute Colportage Association, 1912), 70.
18. Evans, *Great Doctrines*, 70.

WEEK 3—RUTH: A WOMAN WHO LOVES RADICALLY

1. *Holy Land Illustrated Bible: A Visual Exploration of the People, Places, and Things of Scripture* (Nashville: Holman Bible Publishers, 2020), 345.
2. Carolyn Custis James, *The Gospel of Ruth: Loving God Enough to Break the Rules* (Grand Rapids, MI: Zondervan, 2008), 44.

3. Lisa Sharon Harper, *The Very Good Gospel: How Everything Wrong Can Be Made Right* (New York: WaterBrook, 2016), 6.

4. Morgan Hines and Bill Keveney, "Alex Borstein's Powerful Emmys Speech Grabs Attention: 'Step Out of Line, Ladies,'" *USA Today*, updated September 23, 2019, https://www.usatoday.com/story/entertainment/tv/2019/09/22/emmys-alex-borstein-tells-grandmas-holocaust-story-survival/2415239001/.

5. Kevin Love (@kevinlove), Instagram post, July 28, 2021, https://www.instagram.com/p/CR4JHEeNPpg/.

6. James, *The Gospel of Ruth*, 65.

7. Blue Letter Bible, "Lexicon: Strong's H7138—*qārôḇ*," accessed February 8, 2022, https://www.blueletterbible.org/lexicon/h7138/esv/wlc/0-1/.

8. The footnote to Ruth 2:17 (esv) explains that an ephah equals roughly twenty-two liters (which is twenty dry quarts).

9. Inch Calculator, "Quarts to Pounds & Ounces Conversion Calculator," accessed February 8, 2022, https://www.inchcalculator.com/convert/quart-to-pound/. This is the most helpful calculator I found, as it takes the ingredient you're measuring (in this case, barley) into account.

10. As noted in James, *Gospel of Ruth*, 112. James cites Robert J. Hubbard Jr., *The Book of Ruth*, New International Commentary on the Old Testament (Grand Rapids, MI: Eerdmans, 1988), 179 for this information.

11. Blue Letter Bible, "Lexicon: Strong's H6153—*'ereḇ*," accessed February 8, 2020, https://www.blueletterbible.org/lexicon/h6153/esv/wlc/0-1/.

12. Emily Foreman, *We Died Before We Came Here: A True Story of Sacrifice and Hope* (Colorado Springs: NavPress, 2016), 78, italics in the original.

13. Foreman, *We Died Before*, 171.

14. Robert L. Hubbard Jr, *The Book of Ruth*, New International Commentary on the Old Testament (Grand Rapids, MI: Eerdmans, 1988), introduction.

15. You can learn more about this in my study *Leading Wherever You Are: 7 Weeks in the Book of Joshua* (Colorado Springs: NavPress, 2020).

16. Chuck Missler, "The Kinsman-Redeemer," Koinonia House, December 1, 2006, https://www.khouse.org/articles/2006/683/.

17. David Guzik, "Ruth 4—The Marriage of Boaz and Ruth," Enduring Word Bible Commentary, accessed February 8, 2022, https://enduringword.com/bible-commentary/ruth-4/.

18. James, *The Gospel of Ruth*, 185.

19. James, *The Gospel of Ruth*, 203–204.

WEEK 4—BATHSHEBA: A WOMAN WHO CLAIMS HER VOICE

1. "Victims of Sexual Violence: Statistics," RAINN (Rape, Abuse and Incest National Network), accessed February 8, 2022, https://www.rainn.org/statistics/victims-sexual-violence.

2. During the entire Israelite period, the central palace at Lachish stood on an elevated platform overlooking the rest of the buildings and the city gate. See Ronny Reich, "Palaces and Residencies in the Iron Age," in *The Architecture of Ancient Israel: From the Prehistoric to the Persian Periods* (Jerusalem: Israel Exploration Society, 1992), 208; and Robin Ngo, "King David's Palace and the Millo," Biblical Archaeology Society, January 8, 2022, www.biblicalarchaeology.org/daily/biblical-sites-places/jerusalem/king-davids-palace-and-the-millo/.

3. See, for example, Annette Griffin, "Was Vashti Really in the Wrong in Esther's Story?," Bible Study Tools, September 10, 2021, https://www.biblestudytools.com/bible-study/topical-studies/was-vashti-really-in-the-wrong-in-esthers-story.html.

4. Wilda C. Gafney, *Womanist Midrash: A Reintroduction to the Women of the Torah and the Throne* (Louisville, KY: Westminster John Knox Press, 2017), 214–215.

5. See, for example, Jeffery Curtis Poor, "Jesus' Treatment of Women (How He Was Revolutionary)," Rethink, September 23, 2019, https://www.rethinknow.org/how-jesus-gave-women-a-place-and-a-voice/. The following list was influenced by this article.

6. Ben Witherington III, "Mary, Simeon or Anna: Who First Recognized Jesus as Messiah?," Bible Archaeology Society, December 16, 2021, https://www.biblicalarchaeology.org/daily/biblical-topics/new-testament/mary-simeon-or-anna-who-first-recognized-jesus-as-messiah/.

7. Jeffery Curtis Poor, "Jesus' Treatment of Women (How He Was Revolutionary)," Rethink, September 23, 2019, https://www.rethinknow.org/how-jesus-gave-women-a-place-and-a-voice/.

8. Poor, "Jesus' Treatment of Women."
9. Kathy Khang, *Raise Your Voice: Why We Stay Silent and How to Speak Up* (Downers Grove, IL: InterVarsity Press, 2018), 83.
10. Gafney, *Womanist Midrash*, 214.
11. "10. David and Uriah (2 Samuel 11:5-27," from A Study of 2 Samuel, Bible.org, accessed February 15, 2022, bible.org/seriespage/10-david-and-uriah-2-samuel-115-27.
12. Kat Armas, *Abuelita Faith: What Women on the Margins Teach Us about Wisdom, Persistence, and Faith* (Grand Rapids, MI: Brazos Press, 2021), 166.
13. Lysa TerKeurst, "Dealing with Deep Grief," (in)courage, February 27, 2016, https://www.incourage.me/2016/02/dealing-with-deep-grief.html.
14. Blue Letter Bible, "Lexicon: Strong's H5162—*nāḥam*," accessed February 9, 2022, https://www.blueletterbible.org/lexicon/h5162/esv/wlc/0-1/.
15. Malala Yousafzai, in address to the United Nations, New York City, July 12, 2013, malala.org/newsroom/archive/malala-un-speech.
16. Gafney, *Womanist Midrash*, 220.
17. Sara M. Koenig, *Isn't This Bathsheba?: A Study in Characterization* (Eugene, OR: Pickwick, 2011), 87.
18. Gafney, *Womanist Midrash*, 220.
19. Koenig, *Isn't This Bathsheba?*, 89–92.
20. As quoted in Eileen Hoenigman Meyer, "What Is Diversity, Inclusion and Belonging?," Nasdaq, October 21, 2019, https://www.nasdaq.com/articles/what-is-diversity-inclusion-and-belonging-2019-10-21.
21. Gafney, *Womanist Midrash*, 221.
22. Elisabeth Kübler-Ross, *Death: The Final Stage of Growth* (Englewood Cliffs, NJ: Prentice Hall, 1975), 96.
23. Bible Hub, "Commentaries: Proverbs 31:1," accessed February 9, 2022, https://biblehub.com/commentaries/proverbs/31-1.htm.
24. Cynthia Heald, *Becoming a Woman of Strength* (Colorado Springs: NavPress, 2012), introduction, italics in the original.

WEEK 5—MARY: A WOMAN WHO SAYS YES

1. See Scot McKnight, *The Real Mary: Why Evangelical Christians Can Embrace the Mother of Jesus* (Brewster, MA: Paraclete Press, 2007), 11; Sarah J. O'Connor, "Cheating Wives, the Double Standard and a Bizarre Bible Passage," posted in MargMowczko.com on February 18, 2019, https://margmowczko.com/bitter-water-numbers-511-31/; and Tirzah Meacham, "Legal-Religious Status of the Suspected Adulteress (Sotah)," Jewish Women's Archive, accessed February 10, 2002, https://jwa.org/encyclopedia/article/legal-religious-status-of-suspected-adulteress-sotah.
2. McKnight, *The Real Mary*, 19–20.
3. Council of Latin American Bishops, "Final Documents of Puebla," third general meeting of the council, January 1979, footnote to §1135.
4. Edward Sri, *Walking with Mary: A Biblical Journey from Nazareth to the Cross* (New York: Image, 2013), 30.
5. Kat Armas, *Abuelita Faith: What Women in the Margins Teach Us about Wisdom, Persistence, and Strength* (Grand Rapids, MI: Brazos Press, 2021), 60.
6. "The Magnificat," in *Luther's Works, Vol. 21*, ed. Jaroslav Pelikan (St. Louis: Concordia, 1956), 329.
7. On first-century Jewish weddings, see Bruce J. Malina and Richard L. Rohrbaugh, *Social-Science Commentary on the Gospel of John* (Minneapolis: Fortress Press, 1998); and Ritva H. Williams, "The Mother of Jesus at Cana: A Social-Science Interpretation of John 2:1-12," *Catholic Biblical Quarterly* 59, no. 4 (October 1997): 679–92.
8. Sri, *Walking with Mary*, 117.
9. Sri, *Walking with Mary*, 118.
10. Brant Pitre, *Jesus and the Jewish Roots of Mary: Unveiling the Mother of the Messiah* (New York: Image, 2018), 25–29.
11. Pitre, *Jewish Roots of Mary*, 33.
12. Sri, *Walking with Mary*, 127.

13. Pitre, *Jewish Roots of Mary*, 27.
14. Table from *Jesus and the Jewish Roots of Mary: Unveiling the Mother of the Messiah* by Brant Pitre, copyright © 2018 by Brant Pitre. Used by permission of Image Books, an imprint of Random House, a division of Penguin Random House LLC. All rights reserved.
15. Sri, *Walking with Mary*, 73.
16. Sri, *Walking with Mary*, 73.
17. Elisa Morgan, "A String of Yeses," *Our Daily Bread*, accessed February 15, 2022, https://odb .org/US/2019/12/23/a-string-of-yeses.
18. Blue Letter Bible, "Lexicon: Strong's G3600, *odynaō*," accessed February 10, 2022, https://www.blueletterbible.org/lexicon/g3600/esv/mgnt/0-1/.
19. McKnight, *The Real Mary*, 86, emphasis added.
20. McKnight, *The Real Mary*, 86.
21. Blue Letter Bible, "Lexicon: Strong's G80—*adelphos*," accessed February 10, 2022, https://www.blueletterbible.org/lexicon/g80/esv/mgnt/0-1/.
22. McKnight, *The Real Mary*, 96–97.

NavPress is the book-publishing arm of The Navigators.

Since 1933, The Navigators has helped people around the world bring hope and purpose to others in college campuses, local churches, workplaces, neighborhoods, and hard-to-reach places all over the world, face-to-face and person-by-person in an approach we call Life-to-Life® discipleship. We have committed together to know Christ, make Him known, and help others do the same.*

Would you like to join this adventure of discipleship and disciplemaking?

- Take a Digital Discipleship Journey at **navigators.org/disciplemaking**.
- Get more discipleship and disciplemaking content at **thedisciplemaker.org**.
- Find your next book, Bible, or discipleship resource at **navpress.com**.

 @NavPressPublishing

 @NavPress

 @navpressbooks